DOOMSDAY
1917

DOOMSDAY
1917

The Destruction of Russia's Ruling Class

DOUGLAS BROWN

G. P. Putnam's Sons
New York

947.084
B877d

FIRST AMERICAN EDITION 1976

Copyright © 1975 by Douglas Brown

SBN: 399-11615-X

Library of Congress Catalog
Card Number: 75-29002

PRINTED IN THE UNITED STATES OF AMERICA

Contents

List of Illustrations

Preface

Preface

No identifiable event in history has had a more profound effect on mankind than the Russian Revolution of 1917, which has left the world divided ever since between two mutually hostile principles of ordering society.

The political phases of that revolution have been described more often than its social phases. In most history books we read careful accounts of the general state of Russian society in the last years of Tsardom, but after the abdication of Nicholas II the limelight is concentrated on the Bolsheviks' political struggle for power in Petrograd, so that by the time we take our next look at Russian society as a whole we find that all the old landmarks have disappeared.

Yet in February 1917 the *ancien régime* was still nearly intact at all levels except the very top. Things began to happen quickly, it is true, but seldom was there a complete and overnight change of leadership or direction in either the administrative, judicial, military, ecclesiastical, academic, cultural, financial, agricultural or even industrial spheres. The Empire's vast establishment, though decapitated, continued, for a time, and after a fashion, to function. There were thus, in all walks of public life, thousands of members of the old order who still possessed real power, some of whom imagined, indeed, after the fall of an overbearing autocracy, that they wielded greater power than before. In a few months they lost it – to a hitherto submerged race of politicians who worked through an industrial proletariat whose latent strength they alone knew how to mobilize. But at the beginning of the general overturn most of the Old Guard were still at their posts and a sizeable number of them entertained high liberal hopes of a new and democratic Russia. They occupied briefly one of the great watersheds of history, and then slipped off it into oblivion.

One does not need to take a Marxist or determinist view of history to feel that this was their inevitable fate. The shrewdest of contemporary foreign observers, Maurice Paléologue, the last French Ambassador at the Court of St Petersburg, realized as much on the eve of the cataclysm. As an Allied representative during the First World War he was naturally concerned that Russia should stay in the fight, but he saw in her tottering monarchy the one slender guarantee of this, and unlike the British Ambassador, Sir George Buchanan, he had no faith at all in the liberals.

His Italian colleague, Carlotti, believed that if the monarchy were overthrown by a popular rising it would be immediately replaced by a constitutional and democratic regime, in accordance with the programme of the Cadet Party. He thought that, apart from a little bloodshed at the start, the new order would find no great obstacles to its inception.

This was also the view of many socialists at that time, following the theory of revolution as originally propounded by Marx. In their neat scheme of progressive imperatives there were no short cuts. Capitalism had to replace feudalism before, in turn, it was ousted by the dictatorship of the proletariat. Thus, in the confusion that followed the fall of Tsarism there was a brief period in which convinced socialists actually urged the 'bourgeoisie' to assume power. The genius of Lenin was needed to seize the right moment for telescoping history.

Paléologue could not have foreseen this, but he was proved right about the liberals. The abolition of Tsarism, he realized, would inaugurate a period of disorder such as that which followed the death of Ivan the Terrible. And this was because Tsarism was not only the official form of Russian government; it was 'the very foundation, the tie-beam of the Russian community'. Outside Tsarism he saw nothing.

In a famous passage of his memoirs, the French Ambassador drew an English comparison by imagining a successful 20th-century Gunpowder Plot.

'Suppose that at the present time a few English anarchists, using some highly improbable explosive, succeeded in annihilating at one blow King, Ministers, House of Lords, House of Commons, all government departments, police, armed forces and courts of law; in a word, all the machinery of the British constitution. Anyone can see there would be instant and general confusion in the State and a sudden cessation of almost all its vital functions. But it would only be a case of syncope. After a short period of paralysis and amazement you would see public life revived and reorganized by the spontaneous action of provincial and municipal institutions, ecclesiastical bodies, the universities, clubs, chambers of commerce, corporations and those innumerable private associations – religious, political, charitable, philanthropic, literary, scientific and sporting – which swarm on English soil and co-ordinate to a certain extent the free play of individual initiative.

'Such an exhibition of automatic reconstruction is impossible to imagine in a country like Russia, where no manifestation of political or social activity escapes the interference, supervision or strangling grip of the central authority, and the whole life of the nation is the slave of an omnipotent bureaucracy . . . My conclusion is that if Tsarism collapsed, it would bring the whole Russian edifice down with it in its fall. I even wonder whether national unity would survive; for by what force, or in virtue of what principle, could the belt of subject races be kept in place which the traditional policy of the Tsars has girt about the Muscovite State? Would it not mean the end of Russia?'[1]

In the event, Russian forces of reconstruction soon appeared from below the surface, to erect a new central authority and bureaucracy to which the epithet 'omnipotent' could much more aptly be applied than to the fumbling administration of the Tsars. But the old order was not a phantasm merely because the State controlled it. Tsarist

Russia, too, had her provincial and administrative institutions, her Church, her universities, as well as a bewildering
variety of private associations, and they were all the more
fascinating for being Russian. They did not, it is true,
spontaneously react to the death of the monarchy, for the
reason that Paléologue foresaw, but at that moment of time
they existed, and it is worth-while to examine the manner of
their disappearance.

Konstantin Paustovsky has described one obvious aspect
of this interim phase, which, quite apart from the territorial
survivals of the old order made possible by the Allied interventions and the civil war, persisted in Moscow itself for
some months after the Bolsheviks seized power. In spring 1918
'life hadn't settled down yet. The most unlikely people
rubbed shoulders. They were more noticeable than before.
The Revolution had brought them to the surface and shaken
them up – as when you shake a barrel of standing water,
and all the grains of sand, leaves, twigs, beetles and grubs
swim up and rush around on the eddy, meeting and colliding,
until once again they sink and settle down on the bottom.'[2]

Suddenly the speculative thought of decades was being
put to the test. Reactionaries, liberals and revolutionaries
were equally at a loss. So it was a crowded canvas, shared by
the new men with those on their way out – grand dukes and
nobles, society hostesses, generals, judges and bishops, provincial governors and civil servants, millionaire industrialists
and bankers, academics and creative artists, who were still
trying, in their various ways, to hold the body corporate of
Russia together. It was a false dawn and it was a sunset;

'it was the best of times; it was the worst of times'.

And, as might be expected, at such a confluence in history
there were many strange emanations of the human spirit, as
the old and the new jostled in a lurid *danse macabre*.

It was not all gloom and uncertainty, not all a wasteland
of growing fears and frustrated hopes. Though a sense of
doom was always present, there were moments of gaiety
within the impending tragedy. If the scenery included prison
cells and lonely places of execution, there were also the

drawing-rooms, clubs, theatres, smart restaurants and country houses where the old Russian life was flickering to its close.

What greater contrast could there be than that between the gay and decadent world of St Petersburg, under the illusory protection of the double-headed eagle, and the relentless application from below of the stark theories of Communism? When these two elements briefly coincided, some extraordinary kaleidoscopic patterns resulted. Ephemeral as they were, they were an essential step in 'the long march of Everyman'.

Russians, after all, whether on Chekhovian verandahs or in Siberian or European exile, had probably given more thought to the possibilities of revolution than any other people. This grand theme had informed the writings of such giants as Tolstoy and Dostoievsky, it became the groundswell of the music of Stravinsky and Prokofiev and it illumined the theatrical décor of Benois and Bakst. There was a wealth of creative work that spanned the abyss and survived the deadly prostitution of art on the farther side. If the archetypal breach had to come somewhere, there was a certain poetic justice in its appearance not, as the pundits expected, in the industrial West, but in soulful, agonized, introspective Russia.

There is no moral to all this, except the obvious one that when the forces of history come together to produce a great explosion, neither reaction nor liberal idealism can prevent it from taking place. Nor is any society immune from this cosmic possibility – neither that of the present-day Soviet Union, nor our own.

This book is by no means another history of the Russian Revolution. There are many aspects of that apocalyptic event, and many of its crucial episodes, that it either ignores or touches on only in passing. In particular, the fascinating and intricate story of the conversion of revolutionary theory into practice, through the genius of Lenin, does not form part of its theme. The book is merely an attempt to picture the effect of the Revolution on the ruling classes who were swept away by it and either were killed, escaped into exile, or sank into what was to them a completely alien society.

There were estimated to be three million of them, and before 1917 they had, at various levels, conducted the affairs of one-sixth of the terrestrial land-mass. Their experience was unique in history.

* * *

Until 1 (14) February 1918, when the Bolshevik Government adopted the Gregorian calendar used by the western world, Russian dates were thirteen days behind our own. This has been a frequent source of confusion, and I have thought it best to follow Trotsky's practice and use the Old Style dates for the appropriate period, adding the New Style dates in brackets only when some international significance is involved. The February Revolution, March socialists, the April Theses, the July Days and the October Revolution have become too much part of the vocabulary of history to be assigned to different months.

It should be noted, however, that the new State's first May Day was celebrated on what to it was 18 April 1917, as a gesture of solidarity with international socialism.

In the matter of the transliteration of Russian proper names I have followed no consistent plan, but have adopted the forms, 'consistently inconsistent', likely to be most familiar to the English reader.

DOOMSDAY
1917

1

The Process

The Empire over which Tsar Nicholas II was called upon to rule was the largest contiguous area in the whole story of mankind to be subjected to a single government. Comprising a sixth of the land surface of the globe, it linked Germany with Japan, and the Himalayas with the Arctic. It marched with Scandinavia, Western Europe, the Balkans, the Near East, Persia, India and China; and by reason of Alaska, it was even neighbour to the United States.

By what kind of people, before the Revolution, was this immense territory administered? Its subject races included not only wild Tartars and Mongols but civilized Finns and elegant Poles. Yet Great Russia itself, the heart of the Empire, was a land which we should today call under-developed, dependent on foreign capital, in which a tiny ruling class held sway over the mass of the 'dark people' sunk in illiterate and superstitious squalor.

The development of the Muscovite monarchy, leading to the recruitment of a 'serving nobility', or feudal bureaucracy, by Peter the Great, has lent great colour to the Marxist, or class-warfare, view of pre-revolutionary Russian history. Right up to 1917, the citizens of most of European Russia were legally divided into the three estates of nobles, townsmen and peasants, while Peter's Table of Ranks remained in force, whereby half the educated community, civil as well as military, were to be seen constantly in uniform, according to their degree. The suppression of these distinctions, except formally, on the morrow of the February Revolution has usually been interpreted as symbolizing the triumph of the bourgeoisie over feudalism, just as the suppression of the rights of property after the October Revolution has been taken to mark the triumph of the proletariat and the peasantry over the bourgeoisie.

A less doctrinaire view of these two events would see in the former merely the political prelude to the latter. The political revolution swept away the Autocracy and part of the bureaucratic structure that supported it. In so doing it opened the way for the real overturn eight months later, but in itself, except in so far as it produced a great deal of anarchy, it was not socially far-reaching. Only as newly released forces welled up from below, eroding the rights of property, did the old structure finally collapse.

Tsarist Russia, indeed, by the time Nicholas II ascended the Throne, was far from being the crowned monolith of orthodox Marxist belief. After a succession of agrarian reforms it had ceased to be distinctively feudal. Commoners could purchase estates and become landowners, or they could rise in the civil service and armed forces and become noblemen; equally, noblemen could lose their fortunes and social status. The forms were still aristocratic, but the substance was largely capitalist. Among the propertied classes a bewildering variety of social functions was being performed within the traditional structure. Sons of ex-serfs had become exploiting peasants and even millionaires; entrance to the universities, which could no longer be restricted to the nobility, produced the peculiar Russian phenomenon of a classless intelligentsia; there were the 'conscience-stricken noblemen', sometimes described as 'public men', busy establishing a parallel administration on local levels; and there was the 'third element', consisting neither of landowners nor of administrators, but of doctors, teachers and agronomists, who were devotedly working for the betterment of rural society.

All this activity was not the true product of a class struggle. An administration does not form a class in the Marxist sense,

Moscow, February 1917, Soldiers gather in the streets as a sign of solidarity with the rebelling people

An engraving by M. Rashevsky of the environs of St Petersburg

A Georgian nobleman's family at home

A bread queue in Petrograd, February 1917

though it must depend on one. The Tsarist administration did not depend on the gentry alone, though they provided most of its higher personnel. It depended on the generality of the well-to-do, whose economic interests it protected. Social distinctions among them loomed large before the Revolution, partly because of the formal relationship between the nobility and the bureaucracy, but they vanished overnight when the Throne toppled. No one then cried: '*À bas les aristos*'. All wealthy people were lumped together as *burjois*. The propertied classes were a ship's company afloat on the dark sea of the masses, and when the storm broke, captain, officers and first- and second-class passengers all went down with the ship.

Thus the 20th-century political conflict between the liberals and the Government was not historically fundamental. If the Autocracy had conceded a genuine parliamentary constitution the ultimate fate of Russia would have been the same. There would have been a brief period of freedom of speech, writing and assembly, trade unions would have been fully legalized, and the power of the secret police would have been curtailed, but the vulnerability of the new democratic regime, in which the haves would still have attempted to control the have-nots, would have equalled that of the old autocratic one.

Doubtless it was galling for the non-noble and non-official wielders of economic power in Tsarist Russia to be excluded from any formal share of political power at the centre. They were deeply critical of the Government's inadequacies, but unconscious of their own. They felt themselves to be competent adults confined to the political nursery. As committeemen and ideologues they had more to offer the State than the State would accept. In this unnatural situation it was inevitable that they should confuse their relatively minor disabilities with the sufferings of the masses. Yet with those masses they had little contact, and, whether as Slavophiles evoking the soul of Mother Russia or as westernizers obsessed with paper constitutions, they were totally unfitted to lead them.

The idealistic Dr Astrov, in Chekhov's *Uncle Vanya*, told the old children's nurse Marina of his thoughts when a railway signalman on whom he was about to operate died under chloroform.

'My conscience began to worry me as if I had killed him deliberately. I sat down, closed my eyes – just like this – and started to think. I wondered whether the people who come after us in a hundred years' time, the people for whom we are now blasting a trail, would remember us and speak kindly of us? No, Nanny, I'll wager they won't!'

Galina von Meck, grand-daughter of Tchaikovsky's patroness and daughter of a liberal-minded railway magnate who was first employed and then killed by the Bolsheviks, lived to see this prophecy come true, in much less than a hundred years. Looking back, however, after terrible experiences of her own, she denied the Chekhovian impression that all educated liberals were weaklings who let their emotions get the better of them. 'Russia was not populated by such people alone. Many people worked, achieved, "reached Moscow" if they wanted to, created and did positive work. My father was an outstanding figure, but there were others.'

The attempted revolution of 1905 had lent a certain actuality to liberal dreams. Real blood was spilt then, and the whole Empire came virtually to a standstill; as a result the frightened Autocracy conceded a bogus constitution. But what the liberals failed to understand, or at least to accept, was that the motive force in that fateful year came not from them but from below. The four Imperial Dumas in which they sat and expended so much breath were irrelevant to the main course of history. The effective time-bomb was ticking underground.

It might have been thought that Russian society was so stratified, and Russian administration so authoritarian, that the Empire provided an unfavourable climate for the development of socialist theory. In fact the opposite was the case. The stratification of society produced many misfits, who felt they belonged properly to none of the nominal estates of the realm; they became the revolutionary intelligentsia. The authoritarian regime gave no opportunity to these elements to practise legitimate politics in the circumstances, for example, that gave birth to the Labour Party in

Britain; they were therefore thrown back, whether in exile or at home, on an elaborate theorizing about revolution which, diverse as it was, had a very practical application in the period of anarchy that followed the final collapse. The 'dress rehearsal' of 1905 had not been in vain.

All this went on under the eyes of the police, who, after their wont, were more concerned with tumults than with ideas. The ideas could not be put into practice, except in the shape of assassinations, *jacqueries* and strikes. Thus, no official distinction was made between the various revolutionary groups, all agitators being classed as 'anarchists', a name which later came to have a much more precise meaning. The ideology of the future was being crystallized beyond the understanding of the authorities, or, for that matter, of the visionary liberals.

Those doctrinal Marxists who expected a full-scale 'bourgeois' revolution in Russia to precede the seizure of power by the workers and peasants were deceived, not only by theoretical considerations, but by a misapprehension of the true nature of the liberal war of words. Lenin, on the other hand, knew that the Russian middle classes were too small and immature to be capable of filling the gap left by the Tsarist administration. He therefore proposed no alliance with them, but was content to wait until pressure from below thrust them into the front line of politics, where they could easily be picked off and destroyed.

This Bolshevik assessment involved the formation of a small and closely-knit party able to control and direct the general revolutionary movement. The Mensheviks were in favour of a united front under a more diffuse leadership. Both these groups claimed allegiance to the Social Democratic Party, which was the parent of Soviet Communism and in no way resembled the reformist parties in the West which have since borrowed its name.

In the chaos that followed the collapse of Tsarism, the more determined Bolsheviks were bound to win. But first they had to overcome the reluctance of the workers of Petrograd and Moscow to accept the responsibilities of power. This reluctance was due, not only to a too-rigid application of Marxist theory, but to a patent fact of Russian life – that no successful revolution could occur without the support of the peasantry, who formed ninety per cent of the population. Indeed, if the Social Democratic Party was the parent of Soviet Communism, the much larger Social Revolutionary Party (the S.R.s), with its rural base and petty-bourgeois leadership, and its Nihilist tradition, was the natural guardian of most revolutionary dreams.

The experience of 1905, when a largely peasant army, returning from the Japanese war, had failed to mutiny in support of the rising of urban workers, was interpreted in different ways by the two wings of the Social Democratic Party, the Mensheviks and the Bolsheviks. The former were confirmed in their view that the bourgeoisie were more militant than the peasantry, and must be left to take the first revolutionary steps. The latter saw that the peasants must be converted into allies. As a small urban group they could not directly influence the countryside, but they encouraged the development of a left wing among the Social Revolutionaries. After the October Revolution this group was absorbed by the Bolsheviks, while the right-wing S.R.s and the Mensheviks were both suppressed.

The Russian *mujiks* were not politically aware, but they held a passionate belief that the land belonged to those who tilled it. The abolition of serfdom by the 'Tsar-Liberator' Alexander II had in some ways worsened their wretched lot. Their legal status had been improved, but the land available for their use had been actually reduced and encumbered by a debt to be collected over the years to compensate the landlords. This introduction of a money economy was intensified when Stolypin abolished the ancient *mir*, or communal village ownership. Rural life in Great Russia, hitherto static apart from the occasional local revolt, was bedevilled by new inequalities. Some peasants became rich and some landlords poor, but the general standard of living remained as low as ever. The result was a great land-hunger, and a reinforcement of the belief that one day, either by an act of the Tsar or by some mysterious decree of providence, the emancipation would be completed.

This bucolic faith had been the seed-bed of 19th-century Nihilism, with its pointless assassinations, and of Populism, with its romantic hopes. But it was Lenin who harnessed the explosive force to consummate the October Revolution. The liberals had stalled on the agrarian question and the right-wing S.R.s and the Mensheviks hoped it could be solved politically without upsetting the country's economy. Lenin, who was turning that economy upside down, simply offered the peasants their illusory prize, thereby destroying their dream for ever and condemning them to a nightmare of collectivization, famine and migration.

One Marxist dogma was quickly disproved by the Russian Revolution. 'Socialism in one country' was shown to be possible; it was not necessary to await an overturn of the whole world order. There were a few months, after the collapse of the Central Empires, during which the failure of the German working class to seize permanent power seemed to sound the doom of Russian Bolshevism. Then Lenin and Trotsky saw a new way forward. Russian nationalism was restored to the former dominions of the Tsar, and internationalism was converted into imperialism. In many ways the play to be performed under Stalin was a new and more violent version of the old one, but with a totally different cast.

Under the Double Eagle all this was hidden in the womb of time. The political leaders of the workers were for the most part either in prison or exiled, and the peasants had as yet no true leaders of their own, only sympathizers. The explosion was certain to be violent when it came, but until the right spark was ignited a deceptive kind of stability prevailed. The subsoil heaved, but, after 1905, there were no really serious tremors. Since it was impossible to adapt the antiquated superstructure to forces yet unknown, it retained a bizarre rigidity which, when the hour struck, caused its spectacular collapse.

2

Men of Property

At the time of the February Revolution there were thought to be two million nobles in Russia. This may sound preposterous, but the situation, in some respects, was not altogether unlike that in England. There, too, in spite of the Industrial Revolution, there had been a fairly large class, known as the gentry, culturally distinguishable and based historically on landownership, whose more prominent members, at petty and quarter sessions and the like, had been charged with responsibilities of local government. There, as in Russia, the majority of this class had been untitled.

The great difference was that in Russia the whole class formed a legally constituted entity. There was no primogeniture and no hereditary House of Lords, and any titles were transmitted to all legitimate descendants, male or female. But one either belonged to the nobility or one did not. There were rich merchants, with a hierarchy of their own, who were quite happy to be commoners, but the nobility supplied the framework of the State bureaucracy, just as the bureaucracy provided recruits for the nobility. A commoner who attained the rank of major in the army, or its equivalent in the civil service, was automatically ennobled, and with a few further promotions his nobility could become hereditary.

It was Peter the Great who transfigured feudalism by turning it into a State service. The early boyars were a threat to the Throne, but Peter disarmed them by converting them into bureaucrats and letting down a ladder, the Table of Ranks, whereby others could aspire to join them.

The abolition of serfdom in 1861 undermined the agrarian basis of the nobility. Badly managed estates were no longer profitable, and many of them were broken up and sold to the rising class of rich peasants and townsmen. Many nobles sank into genteel poverty, or were lost to sight altogether in the mass of the populace. But the legal entity of the order of nobles remained, and, though its members were eventually relieved of their obligation to serve the State, Alexander II gave them a leading role in rural administration. The peasants had a small share in the election of the local authorities, but only nobles could preside over them. Here again there was a certain parallel with England, where, after the establishment of elected county councils, the squirearchy became less powerful as magistrates but were still expected to take the lead in parish and county affairs. The chief difference was that in Russia there was constant intervention from the centre, in the shape of 'land captains' representing the Ministry of the Interior. A certain tension arose, which sometimes put local noblemen on the radical side in politics. The Social Revolutionary Party, which became legal under the constitution of 1905, was not without support from members of the landowning or ex-landowning class.

The system of titles in Russia was as anomalous as in Britain. 'Prince' was the only native title, and belonged properly to descendants of the once semi-independent boyars. But from the time of Peter the Great it was conferred on favoured individuals, and after the annexation of the Caucasus it was accorded to important Georgian chiefs and later to certain great Armenian and Tartar families. Since it was transmitted to all descendants, there were about two thousand princes in Russia at the time of the Revolution, of every degree of wealth and social standing.

Peter the Great introduced the ranks of 'count' and 'baron', without even troubling to translate these titles from the German. The former was awarded freely, so that by

1917 there were as many counts as princes. Barons, however, were rare in Great Russia, since this style was usually reserved for foreign-born bankers and industrialists, including even Jews, who, as economically important newcomers, needed a handle to their names to establish themselves in St Petersburg society. The Baltic barons, descendants of the Teutonic Knights, resented this dilution of their own particular distinction.

But the vast majority of noble families were untitled, and these included some of the most ancient and illustrious. Upper-class Russians were very conscious of pedigrees, to which they attached more importance than to titles. There was something very English about that too.

The merchants had guilds and ranks of their own, as well as responsibilities for local government in the towns. Those of high culture yielded little in social status to corresponding members of the landowning class, and since 1861 many of them had acquired country estates themselves.

Social mobility operated among the merchants as much as among the nobles. A better-off peasant or a successful *petit bourgeois* might contrive to send his son to university, and so set him on the civil service ladder which, with luck, might bring him noble rank; but the father would be more likely to use his capital to enter the retail or wholesale business, and so qualify for one of the merchants' guilds.

The top rank of industry was enslaved to foreign investment, but economic nationalism was not totally absent from the scene. An Association of Industry and Trade had been founded in 1906 with the object of modifying Russia's colonial status as a convenient market and source of cheap primary products for the West. Curiously foreshadowing the future economic policies of the U.S.S.R., it called for the extension of industrial production, for austerity in consumption meanwhile, and even for rudimentary five-year plans. It urged the irrigation of Turkestan for growing cotton, the better exploitation of the Magnitogorsk iron deposits and the construction of a canal between the Volga and the Don.

The Association was unpopular with conservative landlords because it aimed at weaning away more peasants from the land, with liberals because of its *dirigiste* attitude, and with the Left because of its identification of progress with increased power for private industry. It complained that it received little support either from the Government or from progressive elements in the Imperial Duma. But the real reason for the comparative failure of its programme of economic reform was the inadequacy of the middle class needed to carry it out. On the eve of the First World War the Association confessed in a published report:

'We cannot dwell for long on the reasons why Russia has not shared the general evolution of other countries; the responsibility for that lies in the isolation from the whole world in which Russia lived for so long. The main point is that the inexorable requirements of life have not made possible the building up of that new social stratum which should have been the instrument of the future development of the country.'

As an economic historian, Ruth Amende Roosa, put it: 'In a moment of unaccustomed introspection, Russia's upper business class composed its own epitaph.'

This whole ruling society, though regulated and formalized by law, was in practice highly variegated. In it, great wealth existed side by side with genteel poverty, and, while some hopeful members were climbing the ladders it provided, others were dropping out. The formal rigidity of the system produced its own rebels. Where political development is impossible, short of revolution, where censorship is troublesome and where the right of association is so restricted as to drive many unofficial organizations underground, those who do not mentally accept the *status quo* necessarily occupy a special position in a society that does not absorb them. In withdrawing themselves from it they become conspicuous. Hence the peculiarly Russian phenomenon of the intelligentsia regarded not as an ornament of society but as a revolutionary element within it.

The Russian intelligensia was drawn from every class but transcended them all. It was the active element in an otherwise atrophied community, and to it belonged not only Nihilists and drawing-room liberals, but world-famous writers, musicians and painters. To officialdom all were dangerous, and all had a terrible fascination. Speculative talk, and there was much of it, was invariably, in one sense or another, revolutionary, and it was heard as much in the frivolous shadow of the Court as among dedicated socialists.

After the 1905 insurrection, Countess Kleinmichel spent a period in the country when her only society consisted of bailiffs, managers of sugar refineries and engineers. In a letter to her friend Madame Vera de Talleyrand she wrote: 'Most of them are very well bred people, but their children are abominable. In every one of these families I see a little Marat of fourteen, or a Théroigne de Méricourt of thirteen. It is very disquieting.'[1]

As in France during the reign of Louis XVI, a powerful leaven was at work. It was destructive, and destined to set into permanent shape only under a new race of Jacobins. Everywhere there was a sense of unease. Neither the bureaucracy, the squirearchy nor the small middle class rested on secure foundations, and even the appearance of stability was lacking. The State was ubiquitous, but the nation formless.

In Western Europe towns were compact, treasuring their ancient charters; industrial regions had been subjected to some kind of planning; and villages, with church and manor house, seemed to have grown out of the soil. On the vast Russian plains there was little to hold the eye. Towns, composed of one-storeyed wooden dwellings, straggled unpaved, occasionally dominated by a kremlin, and villages were collections of earthen or wooden huts. Roads were mere tracks, muddy, dusty or frozen according to the season. Prominent alone were the onion-domed churches and, occasionally, a rich man's home, porticoed and aloof, like a planter's bungalow.

Turgeniev has described this empty scene, and the human emotions alive within it. Chekhov has immortalized the life of the country house, at once provincial and rootless, westernized and remote. The heartland of Russia was the most curious kind of colony, whose colonizers knew no home country, except in their dreams.

Maurice Paléologue thought that no society was so prone to *ennui* as the Russian.

'I notice it every day. Indolence, lassitude, torpor, bewilderment; weary gestures and yawns; sudden starts and impulses; an extraordinary facility for easily tiring of everything; an insatiable appetite for change; a perpetual craving for amusement and sensation; gross extravagance; a taste for the freakish, and showy and crazy excesses; a horror of solitude; the perpetual exchange of purposeless visits and pointless telephone calls; fantastic immoderation in religious fervour and good works; facile indulgence in morbid imaginings and gloomy presentiments.'[2]

The monarchy provided the only historical justification for the Empire, and the monarchy had become a sign of contradiction. It was difficult to conceive of Russia without it, but even more difficult to imagine that so archaic an institution could long survive.

Nicholas II was the most powerful ruler of his time, in the sense that his word was law in a sixth of the territory of the world; yet he was singularly ill-served by the people available to carry out his commands, whether they were the over-privileged bureaucrats of St Petersburg or the venal and impoverished officials at the bottom of the ladder. His semi-divine office attracted a superstitious reverence seldom exceeded elsewhere; yet the politically active part of the nation, both above and below the surface, was almost unanimously opposed to him.

The life of the Court reflected these paradoxes. The monarchy's spiritual strength derived from Moscow and the old Russia of Byzantine tradition; yet the Emperor clung to that most un-Russian of cities, St Petersburg, whose 18th-century elegance had been copied from the West. There, however, the civilizing spirit of Catherine the Great had been entirely lost, for in the 20th century the Russian Court, though undoubtedly the most opulent of its time, was culturally among the most banal. Foreign visitors were naturally fascinated by a display of barbaric splendour in a setting of western refinement, but it was nothing more than a *mise-en-scène*; there was no life of the spirit behind it, and no patronage of the contemporary arts above the level of Fabergé's exquisitely vulgar 'Easter eggs'.

Count Valentin Zubov noted this when, as director of the

museum in the former Imperial Palace of Gatchina at the time of the fall of Kerensky, he was able to save many priceless objects from marauding Bolshevik troops, simply because their owners had not realized their value.

'The last generation of the Tsar's family,' he wrote, 'lacking all artistic sense whatever, had shifted works of fine art to the service quarters while they decorated the walls of their own rooms with picture-postcards and portraits of beauties clipped from illustrated magazines.'

Among the objects being moved for safety from Petrograd to Moscow in September 1917, were some from the Dowager Empress's Anchikov Palace. These caught the eye of Count Lucien de Robien, of the French embassy, who remarked that it was incredible that people who could have had the most beautiful artefacts in the world had surrounded themselves with such bric-à-brac. There were Japanese screens acquired from the bazaars, portraits done from photographs 'such as one sees in concierges' lodges', stuffed monkeys under glass domes, and 'the most hideous furniture'. He saw 'a ravishing 18th-century terracotta statuette with a wonderful patina mounted on a pedestal of parrot-green plush'.[3]

Life for the Tsar's own family was one of cosy domesticity interrupted by splendid but meaningless ceremonial. Military reviews, court balls and State receptions followed an invariable pattern, supported by an establishment of a size unmatched in the rest of Europe. The Minister of the Imperial Court had under his command fifteen great officers of state bearing such titles as Grand Chamberlain, Grand Marshal, Grand Cupbearer, Master of the Horse and Master of the Imperial Hunt. Below these there were more than 100 serving officials, as well as some 600 chamberlains and gentlemen-in-waiting. The ecclesiastical establishment numbered 22, there were 38 doctors and a military staff of 150, as well as a bevy of 300 ladies-in-waiting of various ranks. Altogether the Court could call on the services of more than 1,500 persons of gentle blood, who were attended, of course, by a host of servants. Suddenly, in February 1917, this formidable body of parasites melted into thin air, and only a handful of faithful friends remained.

Around this synthetic sun revolved lesser luminaries, being

the courts of the Tsar's close relatives, the grand dukes and grand duchesses. All these personages enjoyed immense incomes from the Appanages set aside for the support of the imperial family, and had palaces of their own, either in St Petersburg or in the pleasant towns surrounding it. Collectively they served no useful purpose, although a few of them had interesting hobbies and pursuits. Too many of the men failed in the one duty that they might have been expected to perform, the preservation of the integrity of the Romanov dynasty as the incarnation of the Russian State. They divorced, married divorcées, or otherwise contracted morganatic unions. They would not have been blamed for keeping mistresses, which many of them did, but their public disregard for their dynastic *raison d'être* was all too symbolic of the decay of the whole imperial ethos. The Tsar, whose sense of duty in this respect was impeccable, was deserted by his own family long before the Revolution came.

There were constant rifts within this precious family, arising from idleness and jealousy. Since the official Court was so dull, some of the grand duchesses amused themselves by adding a royal glamour to the literary and artistic life of the capital. The third lady in the land, after the Empress and the Empress Dowager, was the Grand Duchess Marie Pavlovna, German-born widow of the Tsar's uncle Vladimir. She took an intense dislike to her grim fellow-German, the Empress, and showed it by turning her great palace on the Neva into a rival court where, in an atmosphere of borrowed culture and refinement, one was permitted to poke gentle fun at Their Majesties.

Somehow, amid this empty pantomine, a vast empire had to be governed. Here the Tsar was at a distinct disadvantage. He chose his ministers at will, but, in the nature of the case, there was no large reservoir of talent at his disposal. Promotion in Court circles depended largely on birth, seniority, an unadventurous conformity, and, latterly, on the whims of the Empress influenced by the disreputable Rasputin. All the active elements in the State – in the Duma, in industry, in the elected bodies in town and countryside and in the universities – were regarded as members of a not-so-loyal Opposition. Since the ministers were unrepresentative, depending entirely on imperial favour, they never formed a policy-making team, and the Prime Minister exercised no authority over them. They were single figures in relation to the inert administrative machine, reporting individually to the Emperor. Unless they had the talents of a Witte or a Stolypin, and consequently many enemies, they had little chance of responding positively to the challenges of office. In the last two years of his reign, when the country was in the throes of an all-out war, Nicholas had four prime ministers and appointed no less than six men to the crucial post of Minister of the Interior, while a War Minister was indicted for treason. By that time all vital decisions were taken, not even in the Tsar's study, but in the Empress's 'mauve boudoir', under the ominous portrait of Marie Antoinette, and at the instance of Rasputin.

In analysing the character of Nicholas II, his obstinacy, his weakness and his fatalism, one should recognize that the structure of the Russian State laid on him a burden such as only a political genius could have successfully carried. To have assented, in 1905, to genuine constitutional government would have required of him not so much a weak-kneed surrender as an heroic effort to escape from a strait-jacket. Being a very ordinary man he preferred to follow the course traditionally prescribed for him, while uncomplainingly accepting its evident difficulties and dangers. But it was an historical *cul-de-sac*, and he increasingly lost touch with political reality. Personal relationships took its place, and he was singularly unfortunate in the narrow circle provided by his wife and her friends.

There is a paradox about modern royalty. Though its sole justification, where it survives, is the incarnation of the idea of nationhood, considered as a closed profession or *métier* it is as international as Fords or Anglo-American. This circumstance must have seemed particularly anomalous in Old Russia, where throne and state were held to exist in a mystic union under God. Nicholas II was closely related both to the German Kaiser and to the English king, and therefore had family links with two empires which stood in opposition to his, the one as a military power and the other as a pattern of democracy.

After Peter the Great had turned his back on Muscovite exclusiveness and joined the Western European royal club, all the occupants of the Russian throne had married foreigners, usually Germans. This might suggest to the innumerate that the reigning Tsar would be only half-Russian, but it was Pushkin, no less, who mischievously pointed out that after a few generations he would be left with hardly any Russian blood in his veins at all. The alien dilution, in these circumstances, advances by a very rapid progression, from a half to three-fourths, from three-fourths to seven-eighths, from seven-eighths to fifteen-sixteenths, and so on. Even supposing that some remnants of Russian blood were restored to the strain as the process continued, Nicholas II, nine generations later, was probably as un-Russian biologically as the racial minorities over which he ruled.

Whether the knowledge of this disturbed him we have no means of telling, but the circumstance was not out of line with the ambivalent role of the Russian monarchy. When the Empress, in a letter written in English, tried to steel her husband to fulfil his role as Autocrat, she begged him to emulate 'Peter the Great, John the Dread [Ivan the Terrible] and the Emperor Paul'. But Peter and Ivan slew their own sons, and Paul was murdered by his own nobles. The Nihilists were not the only killers the Romanovs had faced, and the possibility of a palace revolution was ever present even in the 20th century.

Where no regular machine of government exists, a *camarilla* inevitably forms round the man at the top, no matter how high-minded he may be. This generates an atmosphere of intrigue which, in the case of Russia, turned the fashionable clubs and salons of St Petersburg into something very different from their equivalents in the West.

The famous Imperial Yacht Club was, it is true, immune from this infection. It had as little to do with public administration as it had with yachting, simply because its membership was confined to high aristocrats who felt themselves to be above the struggle, at least in those august surroundings. In effect, it was a branch of the official Court, whose stiff etiquette it reproduced. It was a formalization of the top of the social pyramid.

Naïve foreigners were deceived about its true function. In 1922 Countess Kleinmichel, in exile, met Aziz Bey, victim of another revolution. In her youth he had been the Sultan of Turkey's military attaché at the Court of St Petersburg; young, handsome and rich, a good horseman and dancer, he had been very popular in society. Now he was old, sick and penniless, but he ventured to ask the Countess whether the Yacht Club still flourished under the new regime. She had to tell him that it had been taken over by the Bolsheviks, and was now used as a government office. 'Allah, is it possible?' he exclaimed. 'That great and powerful club, those people who knew everything, who could do everything, those fine fellows do not exist any more? Then Russia is surely lost.'[4]

More actively important was the curiously named English Club, which had been founded by British merchants in the days of Catherine the Great. By the time Nicholas II came to the Throne, all its foreign members, apart from diplomatists, had been ousted, and it had come to be the point at which the Autocracy made contact with the limited social circles from which it chose its servants of the second rank. In those beautiful red and gold rooms, overlooking the Fortress of Peter and Paul, and hung with the portraits of all the tsars, reactionary elements engaged in Court intrigues and discreetly assisted each other's promotion in the State. It was said that no provincial governor, returning to the capital on official business, would begin his round of the ministries before discovering, at the English Club, the current lie of the land.

The third exclusive club in St Petersburg, the New Club, was composed chiefly of officers of the Guards and younger members of the imperial family. Not being purely hierarchical like the Imperial Yacht, nor the resort of ambitious officialdom like the English, it was the recognized place where political indiscretions could be safely voiced.

The big industrialists and bankers, who would not normally be eligible for any of these three establishments, had one of their own, inappropriately known as the Agriculture Club, or, less politely, as 'the Potato'. It played an important part in the business life of the Empire, and was a noted place for gambling and trencherwork.

There were other clubs, too, with academic, literary or artistic pretensions, where members of all the propertied classes could meet in surroundings congenial to them. The stratification of Russian society was never absolute, and rank was not the only passport to the *haut monde* of the salons and fashionable restaurants.

This, after all, was the Russia where political oppression, by forcing creative energy into individual channels, had brought forth works of genius out of all proportion to the size of the educated population capable of appreciating them. Philosophy, science, literature, music and painting all provided ways of protesting against the inertia of Tsarist politics. As in pre-revolutionary France, members of the tottering regime were avid disciples of the gifted prophets who foretold its doom – Tolstoy, Dostoievsky, Turgeniev, Chekhov, Gorky, Blok. Such brilliance, when reflected in the other arts, produced a false sense of social creativity. At the Moscow Art Theatre, at the Imperial Ballet, and in the superb music conservatoires and lively studios of the two capitals, under the spell of Stanislavsky, Diaghilev or Stravinsky, one could live an impossible dream.

The tension engendered a certain decadence, too; and the rest of Europe, in the last years of the Belle Epoque, was fascinated by Russia's delayed *fin de siècle*. Enterprising foreigners greatly enjoyed the society of St Petersburg. Robert Bruce Lockhart, when he was in the British consular service, discovered that the *haut monde*, though it was very conscious of its own hierarchy, took strangers as it found them. 'If they liked a foreigner they made no difference between an ambassador and a commercial traveller. If the latter were amusing, he would never be out of their houses. If the ambassador was boring, he was left alone.'[5]

Scandals abounded in St Petersburg, facilitated by the social custom that kept fashionable restaurants open all night, to the sound of balalaikas and gypsy violins. The Orthodox Church imposed certain outward observances on the rich, but otherwise had little influence on them. Mystics and charlatans, not metropolitans and bishops, were the spiritual leaders of the time, and their teachings were not always opposed to sexual licence. Rasputin managed to combine his commanding influence over a puritanical Court with rip-roaring adventures in other exalted circles; and, though this duality reached intolerable proportions in the end, it was by no means at variance with the general tone of Russian café society. If life under the chandeliers, in theatre and salon, was one of glittering formality, its extension to the great restaurants, such as the 'Yar' and 'Stryelna' in Moscow's Petrovsky Park, allowed for indulgences that would scarcely have been tolerated so publicly in the rest of Europe.

To western playboys and philosophers alike the ambience created by the tsarist élite had an irresistible appeal. In the early twentieth century it provided the only example of European culture being self-grafted on to something quite distinct from it. Its practitioners were no mere imitators of the West, like Anglophile Indians or the creators of modern Japan. In their own right they were full members of European society, while being also the heirs of a Byzantine culture which had scarcely survived in Greece itself, and which elsewhere, under Ottoman and Hapsburg rule, had been sternly repressed.

Savage as Russian history had been, it was indubitably linked with a common European past, before the Christian empire of Constantine had been divided. After the fall of Byzantium, Moscow laid claim to be 'the Third Rome'. Thus the Tsars were no upstarts like the Kaisers of Bismarck's creation, but peers of the Holy Roman Emperors of the West.

All this was a heady mixture, in which the western element, assisted by the climate, underwent a strange transformation. The cool classicism of St Petersburg assumed one magic quality under snow, and another in the translucent white nights of high summer.

Wealthy Russians travelled extensively in Europe, and were familiar figures in Paris, in the South of France, and at every kind of fashionable spa. Though they spoke perfect French, German or English, and were fully at home in the world in which they moved, they were sometimes thought

to be a little vulgar and over-fond of display. The elegant
Poles, in particular, despised them, in the manner of the
beautiful boy Tadzio in Thomas Mann's *Death in Venice.*

Yet, in this barbaric world of ikons and samovars, of
troikas and Cossacks, there were brilliant pockets of inherited culture and privilege which could scarcely have
come to fruition in a more egalitarian or progressive society.
Some of the industrialized estates in the Ukraine were little
kingdoms in themselves, ruled by Benthamite philosophers.
At Peresash, near Chernigov, for example, the Korostovetz
family presided over a self-contained community which, by its
combination of agricultural forethought and cultural
awareness, attracted visitors from all over Europe.

The owners had replaced all the wooden buildings with
brick ones – stables, barns, hothouses, and cottages for
imported workers from Latvia, Estonia and Bohemia. They
had installed an elaborate distillery, and provided it with
the latest French equipment and a novel compressed-air
pump invented in Germany. Their model dairy was served
by a herd of eighty milch cows. The manor house was surrounded by a park in which were the guest-house, family
vault, ice-house, laundry, poultry yard and fire station. In
the gardens were 115 varieties of roses, imported from England, France and Luxembourg.

A list of the foreign periodicals subscribed to by this one
household reveals the lengths of eclecticism to which educated Russians could attain. The grandmother read the
French papers *Le Petit Bleu, Le Petit Journal* and *Gaulois.* The
boys had *Answers, The Captain, Tit-Bits, Wide World Magazine, Comic Cuts* and *The Comic Paper,* and entered into most of
the competitions arranged by these magazines. For their
English tutor the *Strand Magazine* and *Punch* were provided.
The mother's politically advanced reading included *La
Revue Scientifique, La Revue Bleu, Le Journal de Genéve* and later
even *L'Humanité.* For general reading there came from Eng-
land the *Times Weekly,* the *People* and the *Graphic;* from
France, *Le Temps, Illustration, Figaro, La Nature,* the *Revue de
Paris* and the *Revue des Deux Mondes;* from Germany, *Die
Woche.*

But there was an intellectual austerity about the Korostovetzes which was not shared by all their landed neighbours. More typical of wealthy feudal life was conspicuous consumption. Here is Vladimir Korostovetz's own description of a summer party given by Komarovsky, the local Marshal of the Nobility, on his neighbouring Belozerkovka estate:

'Drinks and refreshments were served continuously in the dining-room, at the open buffet in the ballroom and on the verandah, while four-in-hands, carriages and riders kept arriving through the main gate and stopping at the verandah steps, where the host was waiting to welcome them with the customary hospitable embrace. Just behind him stood his Circassian, clothed in a *burnous* and decorated with a dagger and blank cartridges. The horses would be unharnessed by grooms in bright *rubashkas* and caps ornamented with coloured feathers. From the kitchens there would be a continual stream of boys in picturesque Cossack dress carrying dishes of food into the house, every dish having been first decorated with flowers by the waiting gardeners. Every man among the guests would choose flowers to present to his lady. A military band from Chernigov and a Jewish string orchestra, one in the garden and one in the house, played alternately without ceasing. The two Komarovsky daughters helped to entertain the guests, dancing with them and so making others dance as well; or they would take a party boating on the lake.

'Those visitors who were overtired from their long journey, or had enjoyed the Komarovsky hospitality not wisely but too well, were unobtrusively taken away to comfortable bedrooms and allowed to sleep. In the evening there was a grand supper with much wine. After dark, bonfires would be lit all round the lake.

'Two or three days would pass in this manner, with picnics held in the woods and meadows.'[6]

Landlordism, on the steppes and in the vast cornlands, with few of the restraints that a more coherent society imposes, produced the kind of eccentrics one would have met in 18th-century England. The former possession of serfs had induced in some of the seigneurs a godlike recklessness of behaviour and the indulgence of individual tastes, whether intellectual or purely bucolic, on the grandest scale. But the system was breaking up quite independently of the time-bomb of revolution at work beneath it, and the number of impoverished and bankrupt noblemen was constantly increasing. The axe relentlessly wielded in Chekhov's cherry orchard was an apt symbol of the current economic change.

The commoners who profited from the situation scarcely formed a class but were a varied group ranging from millionaire industrialists, often of foreign origin, who shared in the fashionable life of St Petersburg, through the traditional and conservative merchant body in Moscow, practising the Old Believers' faith, to the freed serfs who, with peasant cunning, came to exercise a village tyranny more graceless than that of their former masters and later, under the name of kulaks, incurred the terrible wrath of Lenin and Stalin.

There were eccentrics, too, among the merchants. Gorky has given us an unforgettable description of his early patron Bugrov, the self-made millionaire, 'a flour merchant, owner of steam-mills, a dozen ships, a flotilla of barges – a sort of independent prince in Nizhny-Novgorod and the surrounding district'. Like many of his kind in Russia – and, indeed, like thrusting, non-traditional people in many countries, including England – he forswore the State religion, and its Old Believer variant, seeming to need a different spiritual justification for his earthly pilgrimage. The sect he belonged to recognized no clergy at all. Though in this respect he was out of favour with the authorities, they did nothing to prevent him from amassing his great fortune, which they considered to be a stabilizing element in the national life. Gorky saw him in 1896 'slap Witte, the Prime Minister, in a friendly way on the stomach at the All-Russian Exhibition, and stamp his foot impatiently at the Minister of the Court, Worontzov'.[7]

Bugrov founded many charities and transformed his native town, Nizhny-Novgorod, the great fair centre on the Volga, into a modern city. He took a succession of his workmen's daughters to be his mistresses, and when he grew tired of them he married them off with handsome dowries. But Bugrov lived simply, and, according to Gorky, 'had an almost religious attitude to labour, a great faith in its inner power, which with time would link people together in one invincible whole to transform our filthy earth into the garden of paradise'.[8] He died in 1910, and so never saw the other side of that vision.

Not all the rich merchants whom Gorky got to know in the days of his early fame were so single-minded. There was, for instance, Mitrofas Rukavishnikov, citizen of Nizhny-Novgorod. This small hunchback with an adolescent's face 'lived like Des Esseintes, the hero of Huysmans' novel, an artificial life, considering it to be beautiful and refined. He went to bed in the morning, rose in the evening, his friends came to see him at night. Among them was the director of the high school, a teacher of the academy for noble maidens, officials from various Ministries. They spent the night drinking, eating, playing cards and sometimes, having invited local beauties of easy virtue, organized small orgies.'[9]

Of such elements, good and bad, gentle and simple, was the thin top crust of Russian society composed. It was not so uniform as its formal categorization by ranks might suggest, nor so united as any precise theory of class struggle must presume. The rigid Autocracy rested on an élite that was in a state of flux; below this élite, and partly penetrating it, was a revolutionary ferment that had acquired a certain purposefulness in the abortive insurrection of 1905. The peasants, the vast majority of the nation, were still an inert mass, the 'dark people', separated by an impassable barrier of custom, speech and dress from the rest of society, and capable only of sporadic and unco-ordinated acts of savagery. But in the Satanic mills, where urban workers slept in squalor beside their machines, the soviets had preserved a shadowy existence; and, as a shadow behind the shadow, and preparing to absorb it, lay the relentless Bolsheviks.

It required only Russia's participation in the First World War to set the earthquake in motion.

3

War

Experts differ as to the historical necessity of Russia's general mobilization in July 1914. Without her participation in the First World War, would the Western Allies have been defeated, and, if so, what kind of accommodation would have been reached between the victorious Central Powers and the Tsar on his crumbling throne?

Whatever may be the answer to these hypothetical questions, there can be no doubt that the German declaration of war brought a real sense of release to all parties and factions in the Tsar's dominions. By the summer of 1914 the social contradictions described in the previous chapter had reached a state of deadlock in which any reshuffling of the pack was welcome to all the players.

Patriotism is a surrogate emotion, under cover of which many different ambitions can be concealed. For some Russians the need to fight for the Empire was the best means of preserving, in response to external pressure, its traditional character; for others it seemed to open up, at long last, the possibility of radical change. All, however, were able, for the moment, to express their desires in the same patriotic terms; all felt that a new dimension had been added to their frustrating struggle, a new possibility, one way or the other, of regeneration. Briefly, and for the only time in his reign, Nicholas II became in truth a Tsar of all the Russias—of reactionary, of liberal, and of revolutionary Russia. He even became the true Tsar of the Poles and the Jews.

The scene outside the Winter Palace, when Nicholas repeated the oath taken by Alexander I at the time of Napoleon's invasion, that he would not make peace before the last foreign soldier had been chased from Russian soil, has often been described. It was the reverse of Bloody Sunday nine years before, when at the same spot the same monarch's troops had mercilessly mown down a procession of peaceful demonstrators. On this occasion, Sir Bernard Pares wrote, 'the vast multitude fell upon their knees and sang "God Save the Tsar" as it had never been sung before'.[1]

What was that motley crowd thinking, to whom the idea of Holy Russia had suddenly become a reality? So far as the subjects of this book were concerned, the privileged minority, whether official or non-official, this new surge of patriotic sentiment must have made them feel, for the first time, that they were fully caught up, as individuals, in a national effort. The Autocracy, it appeared, was recruiting them at last, and turning them into citizens as well as subjects.

And so, indeed, it proved to be. From that time onwards, until the Bolsheviks finally took over, autocratic Russia was to have, by a supreme paradox, more governments than one.

This was the inevitable result of failure at the very top. The Autocracy by itself was incapable of conducting an all-out war, and the unconscious realization of this prevented its higher servants from joining in the patriotic resurgence. Vladimir Korostovetz, by this time an official of the Ministry of Foreign Affairs, remarked on the complacency of the Tsar's immediate entourage. When war was declared he rushed round to the English Club to snatch a hasty supper before tackling the consequent night's work at his ministry. There was little excitement at the news he brought. A few junior members hurried away to report to their immediate superiors in government, but 'the seniors suddenly fell silent, then began to fidget in their seats, and finally started a deliberate discussion as to what appointments and imperial favours might be expected, thus giving the impression that no storm, no matter how threatening, would ever succeed in disturbing their stoical calm'.[2]

Superficially, it is true, the apex of the State pyramid assumed the appearance of being deeply involved in the war effort. The Empress herself, with her ladies, dressed in nurse's uniform, and even underwent some medical training; nor did she spare herself in this symbolic role. The wealthy turned their surplus palaces into hospitals. Princesses sold paper flags in the streets in support of war charities. The next imperial 'Easter eggs' from the house of Fabergé were austerely adorned with the Red Cross, or made of blackened steel and poised on pieces of shrapnel. St Petersburg was boldly renamed Petrograd, and a decree was issued forbidding the speaking of German in public.

In the view of one contemporary diarist, Countess Kleinmichel, the turning of palaces into military hospitals helped to develop the feelings of envy that slumbered in the minds of peasants under arms.

'Nothing is good enough or beautiful enough for Russia's defenders, we used to think; but, though the palaces of the nobility were marvels of sanitation and comfort, town hospitals and those organized by the War Ministry were bad – patients slept in uncomfortable beds and were ill-fed and carelessly nursed. Inequality in luxury is more difficult to bear than equality in poverty. Hatred and envy stirred the hearts of men lying in military hospitals, while gratitude found no room in the hearts of those we sheltered in our palaces. They said malevolently: "It is so that the nobles may live in these palaces that we toil ten hours a day in the fields and factories." '[3]

When the Revolution came, the Countess believed, it was the 'spoilt and fêted' former patients from these palaces who guided the Red bands to pillage them.

However this may have been, it is certain that beneath the patriotic façade a real revolution was taking place. As disaster succeeded disaster at the front, and the abject logistical failure of the War Ministry became apparent, Russia moved for the first time into a period when 'public men', as distinct from officials, played a leading part in national affairs.

Since 1864, Russia had possessed a rudimentary and semi-democratic form of local government. Rural areas had their provincial and county councils, known as zemstvos, and towns their municipal dumas. Until the first Imperial Duma was summoned in 1906 these bodies were considered by liberal elements as the natural seedbeds of future constitutional reform. In the Japanese war a group of them had organized relief for the wounded, though their political ambitions went much further.

Such organizations came into their own in 1914. The problems created by the influx of refugees from the war zone called for an administration which the official bureaucracy was quite unable to provide. Spontaneously, and without any encouragement from the Government, two all-Russian unions were formed, composed respectively of representatives of the zemstvos and of the municipalities. By 1915 these Voluntary Organizations, as they came to be known, with their headquarters not in official Petrograd but in Moscow, had become large-scale purchasers of commodities for the civilian population, and even major suppliers for the army itself. Together they employed thousands of people. Reluctantly the Government had accepted their help, and they were already a powerful factor in Russian public life.

Encouraged by this development, a conference of manufacturers in May 1915 demanded that industry, rather than the Government, should organize the production of arms and ammunition. 'War Industry Committees' were established in every province, and a co-ordinating council, known as the Central W.I.C., was set up in Moscow. A. I. Guchkov, later War Minister in the first Provisional Government, was its chairman, and A. I. Konovalov, a great Moscow industrialist, his deputy.

These three Voluntary Organizations, consisting of the zemstvos, the municipalities and industry, did not formally coalesce, but rapidly assumed the same political character. They inspired the formation of the Progressive Bloc in the Duma, led by the Constitutional Democrats (Cadets), with its demand for 'a Government of public confidence'. But, unlike the Duma, the Voluntary Organizations were not a mere talking-shop and stood in no danger of being prorogued. They were an integral and essential part of the war effort, and almost constituted a parallel Imperial Government.

This organ of state, for it was nothing less, took the un-precedented step of inviting workers in the war industries to send delegates to the W.I.C.s, both provincial and central. The Bolsheviks, following Lenin's principle of non-cooperation with the bourgeoisie, declined the offer, but eventually a Labour Group, composed of Mensheviks and S.R.s, was established at the Central W.I.C., complete with two rooms, its own telephone and funds.

Here was a Socialist Trojan horse, the first in the history of Russia. The Group pursued its special political ends and never fully co-operated with the Committee, but the liberals who sponsored it hoped to use it as a weapon to counteract undue Government pressure while the war lasted, and as a weapon to bring about moderate constitutional change when it was over. The shortlived alliance was based on a common belief that at all costs the Empire must be defended from German aggression; in the one case to preserve a framework for constitutional reform, and in the other to provide an arena for total revolution.

However, in August 1915, after the failure of a half-hearted attempt by some of the less reactionary ministers to persuade the Tsar to form a responsible government, the liberals in the Duma and the Voluntary Organizations began to have doubts whether, even in the event of a success-ful outcome of the war, the Autocracy could be persuaded to abdicate peacefully. In September, therefore, they went deeper into opposition, and, as well as claiming that the Government was incapable of waging the war without their help, spread rumours that it was secretly preparing for a separate peace.

Thus occurred the great rent in the fabric of the Russian wartime establishment which led directly to the destruction of both the Government and its bourgeois opposition. The internecine and suicidal struggle was carried on with great bitterness, though under the double threat of a German victory and a Russian insurrection. The liberals vilified the Government in every possible way. They chose the Empress as the chief 'traitor', calling her *Nemka* (the German woman) in imitation of the French revolutionaries who denounced Marie Antoinette as *l'Autrichienne*. In point of fact the

Muravyev Investigation Committee, set up afterwards by the Provisional Government, found no evidence of treason against any member of the imperial household, and everything one knows about the Empress herself suggests that, though she was of German origin, her extravagant self-identification with the destiny of the Romanovs would have made disloyalty impossible for her. Yet her friend and mentor, the unspeakable Rasputin, provided the opposition with a god-given Aunty Sally, and enabled them to widen the rift within the imperial family itself.

The Government, on its side, though it used secret funds to support the ultra-right-wing press, did not dispose of sufficient talent to effectively counter the attacks of its liberal enemies. Nevertheless, the Voluntary Organizations themselves were not immune from criticism. They were in a position to grant lucrative contracts to individuals, their accounting system was suspect and inefficient, and, as they became a power in the land, they underwent a Parkinsonian expansion rivalling that of the official bureaucracy. Above all, their patronage in the field of reserved occupations turned them into a sought-after means of avoiding active service, so that the *zemgussar* (zemstvo hussar, or draft-dodger, who could still preen himself in semi-military uniform) became a universally despised figure in folk mythology.

Thus the relationship between the Autocracy and the only element in the nation that could have usefully transformed it went sour, causing a split in the establishment which opened the way to revolutionary forces. These forces lacked leadership during the war period, since all the great socialist figures of the future were either abroad or in Siberian exile. But there was no true leadership on the other side either, and the frail envelope of the Russian State, under all the pressures that were developing, was doomed to burst before long.

Most of the high aristocracy stood aloof from this largely middle-class attempt to share in public administration. Their only wartime role was to provide officer sons for the military holocausts in East Prussia and Galicia, where two-and-a-half million Russian soldiers perished. On the eve of the general overturn, the remnants of feudalism failed to rally as a group, except in so far as some of them joined in last-minute abortive plans to save the dynasty through a palace revolution.

Landmarks were changing fast within the propertied classes themselves. The war had produced a new race of speculators and profiteers who spent their money as freely as those with inherited wealth, but with considerably less decorum. Officers for the decimated armies had to be recruited from the radical intelligentsia, to the detriment of regimental tradition and discipline. Social distinctions, at this level, were being rapidly obliterated.

Prince A. Lobanov-Rostovsky, a young lieutenant in the Guards, who was at the front during the winter of 1915-16, noted a clash of views between regular and reserve officers. 'The former had no political views at all. When I happened to mention politics to a regular officer he would look at me suspiciously and reply sharply: "I have no political opinions. I am a servant of the Tsar, and my duty is to obey the orders of my superiors." That put an end to the matter. But with the reserve officers – former engineers, lawyers, actors, mostly university graduates – the case was very different, and they followed the gossip about what was going on at home with passionate interest. An invisible hand seemed to be stirring up trouble. All kinds of rumours were rife concerning the imperial family and particularly their relations with the notorious Rasputin. The Empress was the object of hatred, openly expressed. Aside from the backstairs gossip about her affair with Rasputin, rumours were spread that she was openly favouring the Germans, that a radio station had been found in the palace communicating directly with Berlin, that in visiting hospitals she would stop and talk for hours with German wounded and pass the Russians without a word. As for the Tsar, all kinds of gossip started about his weak-mindedness, his lack of character, and finally a new rumour that he had started drinking heavily.'[4]

Yet his was still the army in which hierarchical conventions had reached the height of absurdity. To a superior officer it was not enough to say 'Yes, sir' or 'No, sir'. One had to say 'Certainly so' or 'In no wise no'. When praised, the proper reply was 'Eager to serve'. To these the correct forms of address had to be added. Officers up to the rank of general were 'High Well-Born', generals were 'Excellencies' and aide-de-camp generals 'Super-Excellencies'. A titled officer was addressed as 'shining' and a prince of ancient lineage as 'becoming brighter'. Of course, with long usage, these forms did not carry a literal significance in the original Russian (any more than in England one 'worships' a mayor or a magistrate), but they militated against the two great military virtues of simplicity and brotherhood. Moreover the custom whereby senior and junior officers messed separately was in itself conducive to the spread of revolutionary ideas among the latter.

The euphoria of 1914 did not last long. One might have thought, however, that even in the presence of military defeat it would at least have been succeeded by a feeling of excitement at the prospect of either resisting or furthering impending change. But that acute observer, Paléologue, noticed a distinct failure of morale among the upper classes, which he attributed in part to the fact that in wartime they could no longer indulge their taste for foreign travel.

'I am not surprised,' he wrote, 'that in persons who once seemed to me perfectly healthy I am always seeing symptoms of weariness, melancholia, nervous debility, mental disorders, incoherence, an unhealthy credulity, strange obsessions and a superstitious and demoralizing pessimism.

'The feature that has struck me most in my conversations with politicians, soldiers, men in high society, civil servants, journalists, financiers, industrialists and teachers is the vague, fluid and inconsistent character of their notions and schemes. There is always a lack of co-ordination and continuity somewhere. The relationship between facts and ideas is hazy; calculations are merely approximate and perspectives blurred and uncertain. Russians see reality only through a mist of dreams, and never have precise notions of time or space.'[5]

Anna Vyrubova, the Empress's ill-chosen confidante, was under the same impression, and she wrote in her memoirs: 'For the hundredth time I asked myself: what has happened to Petrograd society? Are they all spiritually sick, or have they contracted some epidemic that rages in wartime?'[6]

Not that Petrograd, even in wartime, lacked the appearance of gaiety. Vyrubova herself confessed that in no other season were such gowns to be seen as in the winter of 1915–16, or so many diamonds purchased. For those in the know, war profits were there for the taking, as Trotsky expressed it, in his magnificently vulgar way:

'Everybody splashed about in the bloody mud – bankers, heads of the commissariat, industrialists, ballerinas of the Tsar and the grand dukes, Orthodox prelates, ladies-in-waiting, liberal deputies, generals in the front and rear, radical lawyers, illustrious mandarins of both sexes, innumerable nephews, and more particularly nieces.'[7]

True, the city was under partial blackout, for fear of the Zeppelins, and at night the streets were infested by footpads. Because of transport difficulties, the lack of heating fuel during the hard winters was already being felt even by the well-to-do, and the Diplomatic Corps were furious to see coal delivered by army lorry at the rococo palace of the ballerina Kschessinska, the Tsar's former mistress and the Grand Duke Andrei's present one, when they themselves were in short supply. But private receptions were as brilliant as ever. Guards officers were present in peacetime profusion. The Tsar's quixotic prohibition of vodka and other alcoholic beverages at the start of the war had been attended by withdrawal symptoms among the general population, but it scarcely affected the rich who had well-stocked cellars and access to the black market.

The cultural life of the large cities continued unabated. Before the war, individual Russians had achieved worldwide reputations in all the creative arts. The cultural importation from the West, which had begun under Peter the Great and reached its apex under Catherine, had become a two-way traffic, making Russia in the fullest sense cosmopolitan. Now she was isolated from the rest of Europe, and was to remain so until after the break in the blockade in 1922; to this day she cannot be said to have re-entered the free world of the arts. But at the outbreak of the war many leading Russian artists and writers patriotically hurried home from Paris and elsewhere. During the war-time pre-revolutionary period the ballet was at its classical best, and Chaliapin sang.

On the other hand, though experimental art movements in the West between the World Wars had considerable influence in Russia, the Russian school of abstract painting developed in isolation within a closed and angry circle. In February 1915, its rival leaders Malevich and Tatlin came together in Petrograd at a show absurdly called 'The Futurist Exhibition: Tramway V', which was followed in December by '0.10: The Last Futurist Exhibition'. Here occurred the birth of Malevich's 'Supremacist' style, which briefly after the Revolution represented the reigning principle in Soviet art. Meanwhile, at the Moscow Kameny Theatre, Tairov and Alexandra Exter were working on their 'Synthetic' system of stagecraft, in which set, costume, actor and gesture were intended to form a dramatic whole. On the eve of the Tsar's abdication, a Moscow newspaper wrote that the public were more interested in their productions than in the violent speeches in the Duma of the Cadet leader, Professor Milyukov.

Indeed, the bourgeoisie did take a dilettante's interest in these experiments, and rich industrialists helped to finance them. The innovators held exhibitions in aid of war charities, and some, including Mayakovsky, the revolutionary painter and poet, went to the front as war artists.

The general mood, however, was one of despair rather than of expectation. Camilla Gray has compared it with that of the German Dada movement.

'There was the same feeling of uselessness, the same sense of victimization in a hostile, senseless world. The ludicrous masks that the Futurists wore or painted on their faces – in *Victory over the Sun* the actors wore *papier-mâché* heads half as tall again as their bodies, and performed on a narrow strip of stage using marionette gestures to accompany their "non-sense" words – the guy-like costume they adopted, the undignified public brawls and vociferous street language of their paintings and poetry, all these typical Russian Futurist traits indicate a Dada-like rejection of reality, a bitter mocking of themselves as useless misfits in a decadent society. The mood was essentially non-creative, negative, passive.'[8]

It changed and blossomed later, in a blissful dawn, only to be withered for ever by the killer-sun of Stalinism.

This artistic passivity, in the last days of Tsarism, was

Russian officers of the Imperial Army relaxing

A group of merchants from Nizhny-Novgorod taking tea

General Alexeiev (left), Chief of the General Staff from August 1915 until he resigned in May 1917, with A. F. Kerensky, head of the Provisional Government from July to October 1917

General Kornilov, Commander-in-Chief from July 1917 until he was dismissed in August of the same year reviewing troops

exceeded only by the almost total inanition of the governmental machine. The Emperor, who in his bones must have known that only the army could save him, frequently left what he called 'the poisonous atmosphere of Petrograd' for the Stavka (military headquarters) at Mogilev, where there was no serious role to occupy him and he spent much of his time playing dominoes. The wartime army was not the army in which he had been brought up. General mobilization had turned it into a mass of peasants dressed in military greatcoats, and officered, to a considerable extent, by those very idealists of the 'third element' who, consciously or not, had for years been busily undermining the moral basis of the Autocracy. The government of the Empire was left in the hands of the Tsaritsa, neurotic and unbending, whose adoption of the Romanov mystique was little short of paranoiac. Rasputin was murdered by members of the imperial family itself, to the suitable tune of 'Yankee Doodle Dandy.' His place as confidant was taken by the preposterous Protopopov, Minister of the Interior, a man suffering from general paralysis of the insane, whose influence rested on his claim to be in touch with the disgusting *starets* beyond the grave. Protopopov cut the one link between the administration and the masses by arresting the members of the Labour Group on the War Industry Committee.

Since its authority no longer rested on the good will of any of its active citizens, the regime depended for its survival on the day-to-day vigilance of the police, both uniformed and secret. The police, though armed, were not strong enough to deal with a general insurrection, and therefore depended on their ability to call, when necessary, on the help of the military. They did just this in October 1916, when trying to deal with a group of strikers in Petrograd, and found that the rifles of the soldiers were directed not at the strikers but at themselves. The Cossacks, professional riot-quellers, were sent for and they restored order; later 150 of the mutineers were executed by firing squad. Nevertheless, this was the obvious turning-point. The Cossacks, in spite of their independent status, could not be expected to be permanently immune from the mood that was sweeping over Russia, and in any case there were too few of them to hold the whole Empire down. Whoever it was who reported this affair to the Tsar might well have used the Duc de Liancourt's words to Louis XVI after the fall of the Bastille: 'Sire, it is not a revolt; it is a revolution.'

The following January, the Court awoke from its death-sleep and braced itself to go through the motions of receiving a high-ranking delegation of the Allied Powers, sent to prod the Russians into opening a new offensive on the eastern front in the spring of that year. Lord Milner led the British members. All the old splendours came to life for the last time. Banquet succeeded banquet, reception succeeded reception, the chamberlains and A.D.C.s present wearing their glittering decorations. It was a strange experience for the British, French and Italians, accustomed to wartime austerity; stranger still that it produced no military result whatsoever; and strangest of all for those who realized that they were attending Belshazzar's very last feast.

And now, when it was far too late, the high aristocracy, joined by members of the imperial family, decided to re-enter the field of politics and, to save their own skins, plot with the liberals for the replacement of the Tsar by some other Romanov who would agree to constitutional government. They totally misread the situation, because the revolutionary forces, inchoate and leaderless as they were, constituted an element that they and the liberals were quite incapable of controlling. The drawing-room conspiracies, so openly and naïvely conducted, were a form of fiddling while Rome was about to burn.

On 13 January Prince Gabriel Constantinovitch gave a supper for his mistress, a former actress, which was attended by the idle and ill-mannered Grand Duke Boris and a glitter-ing crowd of aristocrats and courtesans. Paléologue was there and noted that the one topic of conversation was the coming palace revolution, which regiment of the Guard could be relied on, when the most favourable moment for the outbreak would be, and so on.

'And all this', Paléologue remarked, 'with servants moving about, harlots looking on and listening, gypsies singing and the whole company bathed in the aroma of Moet et Chandon *brut imperial*, which flowed like water!'[9]

Trotsky diagnosed this behaviour as the death-weariness of a class that has no future: 'As a lamp before it goes out flares up with a bright although smoky light, so the nobility before disappearing gives out an oppositional flash, which performs a mighty service for its mortal enemy.'[10]

History overtook these champagne plots. Nine days later, on Wednesday, 22 February, the Tsar for the last time left his palace at Tsarkoye Selo for military headquarters at Mogilev, and the fact that he was never to return as monarch was the result of something more serious than a palace revolution.

On the following night Paléologue observed traces of anxiety in two of his dinner guests, Trepov, recently dismissed as Prime Minister, and Count Tolstoy, Director of the Hermitage gallery. They were concerned about the supply of food to Petrograd, where the bread queues were ominously lengthening. Most of those present, however, were preoccupied with the brilliant evening party that Princess Léon Radziwill was to give that Sunday, at which there was to be music and dancing. 'Trepov and I stared at each other,' the Ambassador recorded. 'The same words came to our lips. "What a curious time to arrange a party!" '[11]

The sporadic disorders that broke out on the following day did not immediately disrupt the life of Petrograd. They were considered a matter for the police, who had dealt with such incidents before. Neither the majority of Duma members nor the administration recognized at first the full political significance of these events, but by the end of the week people who had no wish to court trouble on the streets preferred if possible to stay at home. On Saturday only about fifty people were present at a concert in the Mariinsky Theatre, and there were gaps in the orchestra. The square outside was desolate; the French Ambassador's car was the only vehicle there. Escorting home the Vicomtesse du Halguoët, his secretary's wife, he observed that the Moika Bridge was guarded by a picket of police and that troops were massed in front of the Lithuania Prison. Madame du Halgouët remarked: 'Are we witnessing the last night of the regime?'

Not quite. The following night Princess Radziwill's party duly took place, the Radziwill palace was brilliantly illuminated, and the carriages outside awaited the highest in the land. A French guest reported a certain lugubrious atmosphere at first. The Grand Duke Boris looked worried as he danced. Nevertheless, 'in spite of everything we actually ended by enjoying ourselves'.

At the English Club, Maklakov, former Minister of the Interior, was recounting to his successor Protopopov, and to Stuermer and Prince Tumanov, an incident which had occurred the previous day in the Znamensky Square, when the Cossacks had not only refused to fire on the revolutionary mob but had attacked the captain of police and cut his head off. According to Vladimir Korostovetz, who was dining at the next table, the news made no impression on them.

'All that one had heard on that occasion had been various demands to the chief steward: "Pavel, a bottle of Lafitte", "Pavel, a bottle of Mouton Rothschild". It struck me that the guests of the English Club were unconsciously holding the funeral repast of the Russian Empire that was declining so swiftly in the red sunset.'[12]

Next day the mutiny was in full swing, and by nightfall the ministers of the Imperial Government, deprived of electric light in the Mariinsky Palace, and rightly fearing that it would soon be sacked by the mob, slipped away one by one and went into hiding. Only a small group of loyal troops, under General Belyaev, the Minister of War, and General Khabalov, commander of the Petrograd military district, was left to guard the Winter Palace. There the Grand Duke Michael, the Tsar's brother, had taken refuge after a day spent in discussions with the dissolving Cabinet and Rodzianko, President of the Duma, about a desperate last-minute plan to save the monarchy. At 3 a.m. His Imperial Highness summoned the two generals and asked them to withdraw their troops, as he 'did not want them to fire on the crowd from the house of the Romanovs'. The force moved to the Admiralty and surrendered their weapons to officials there. Then they dispersed to barracks or to officers' private quarters, to await the uncertain future.

Two days later, in his imperial train at distant Pskov, the Tsar of All the Russias resigned the crown of an empire that no longer existed.

4

February 1917

On Tuesday 21 February 1917, Nikolai Nikolayevich Sukhanov, editor, in his spare time, of Maxim Gorky's paper *Letopis*, was sitting in his office in the Turkestan Section of the Tsarist Ministry of Agriculture.

'Behind a partition,' he recorded, 'two girl typists were gossiping about food difficulties, rows in the shopping queues, unrest among the women, an attempt to smash into some warehouse. "Do you know," suddenly declared one of these young ladies, "if you ask me, it's the beginning of the Revolution!"

'These girls didn't understand what a revolution was. Nor did I believe them for a second. Not one party was preparing for the great upheaval. Everyone was dreaming, ruminating, full of foreboding, feeling his way.

'These philistine girls whose tongues and typewriters were rattling away behind the partition didn't know what a revolution was. I believed neither them, nor the inflexible facts, nor my own judgement. Revolution? Highly improbable. Revolution! Everyone knew this was only a dream – a dream of generations and long laborious decades. Without believing the girls I repeated after them mechanically: "Yes, the beginning of the Revolution." '[1]

The truth is that a revolution steals upon an existing regime like a mortal disease. The final attack opens like

53

others in the past; its early symptoms do not differ from those that have marked the beginning of previous illnesses, from which the patient has recovered.

The citizens of Petrograd were familiar with bread riots and unruly strikes, even in wartime. There was no telling, in February 1917, that the disturbances in the city would not be quickly suppressed by the police, the Cossacks, and, if necessary, the military garrison. Prosperous people, going about their business or attending theatres and evening parties, recounted rumours of disorders in various parts of the capital, but at first they were apprehensive rather than excited or alarmed.

Yet the feeling best expressed in the words 'this is it' spread quite rapidly. The psychological preparation for some great event had affected all classes. At the same time no one, whatever his political views, knew quite how to act. The hurricane, when it came, took by surprise those who had been preparing for it, or arming themselves against it, all their lives.

The basic physical achievement of the February Revolution was the annihilation of the Tsarist police. The wretched 'pharaohs', deprived of the support of the army, were hunted down and killed by the mob, their stations were set on fire and their prisons thrown open. Russia had been a police state. For a space it was that no longer, and an immense vacuum was created.

Power was there to be seized, and at first it was divided between those who, though smarting under the Autocracy, had controlled a complex economy, and the anonymous forces that had destroyed the Autocracy's administrative carapace. This dual regime was shared between a Provisional Government which hoped it could control the Revolution, and the Petrograd Soviet which, though feeling itself unfitted to assume supreme power at once, had no doubt that that was its ultimate destiny.

What must have surprised the liberals was the capacity of the 'dark' forces, which at that time were without effective leadership, to organize themselves in a way that made them, from the very beginning, a decisive power in the new state. All the liberals' democratic ideas were immediately challenged by uneducated people who, in the chaos that followed the fall of Tsardom, were in a position to make demands that seemed to strike at the roots of ordered society.

At the very beginning of the disorders, before the regimental mutinies had changed everything, a group of liberals from the Duma and the Voluntary Organizations had attempted to strike while the iron was hot. In the flat of Kerensky, then a Duma member close to the Social Revolutionaries, they had made tentative contact with a small underground cell of workers and soldiers known as the Inter-District Committee. This, the first meeting on equal terms between the haves and the have-nots of Russia, had proved to be ominously abortive. The Committee, which shared the Bolshevik theory of revolution, had soon revealed that it had no wish to compromise the movement that was developing in the streets of the capital by associating itself with a section of the bourgeoisie.

The disturbances lasted from Thursday 23 February to Thursday 2 March. Those eight days were marked by many savage murders, of serving officers chiefly, and by the destruction of public and private property. The mutinies spread to the navy, not only at Kronstadt but in Reval and Helsinki. There the ratings were not illiterate peasants in uniform but skilled professionals fully capable of understanding the arguments of socialist agitators. Some of their comrades had been imprisoned since 1905. There were forty naval victims, many of whom were hacked to pieces and thrown into the sea. Admiral Neperin was among them, even though he had declared his support for the Revolution. Admiral Viren, at Kronstadt, faced a firing squad and said: 'I have served my Tsar and my country faithfully. It's your turn now. Try to give some meaning to your life.'

These horrors could not compare with those that lay ahead for Russia, but they frightened the new authorities in Petrograd, who had been congratulating themselves that in the street-fighting the casualties had not been above a thousand. As with all revolutions, the actual impact that overturned everything was narrow – a garrison mutiny in February and a local *coup d'état* in October. It was the consequences that were tremendous.

The comparative bloodlessness of the February Revolution was due to the fact that there was so little resistance. Once the Cossacks had gone over to the people there were only the doomed police, fighting for their lives. Officers who were not in barracks at the time stayed at home. So did all the civilian leaders of the city's social and commercial life, whose fate was being sealed. The great factories were on strike or subject to a lockout, the trams had ceased running, there were no droshkies, and private cars were liable to be commandeered. Mutinous soldiers were careering about the streets in stolen vehicles, firing at random at the rooftops where the last of the pharaohs were popularly supposed to be manning their machine guns. Private houses were broken into in the search for these unfortunates, and there was a certain amount of looting.

By the evening of Monday, 27 February, the Admiralty was on fire, documents from the burning Law Courts were blazing in the streets, every police station had been captured, the Astoria Hotel had been looted, and the Fortress of Peter and Paul, the Russian Bastille, had disgorged its collection of political prisoners and criminals.

One can imagine the conflicting emotions in the breasts of a whole host of sorcerer's apprentices. Men of property normally tremble when the police, whom they regard as their friends and protectors, quit their posts. In Russia, however, the police had become so identified with the hated Autocracy that their disappearance was at first welcomed by nearly all classes of the population. The bourgeoisie, as we must now describe the whole of the surviving establishment, whether of noble birth or not, were hoping, while they bowed their heads before the passing storm, for a new political order based on parliamentary democracy, in which they would at last breathe freely but in which their property and investments would be safe.

For the moment, however, they were thoroughly alarmed. Were the Revolution to fail, and were the loyal troops that the Tsar had ordered to march on Petrograd to succeed in scaring the mutinous garrison back into its barracks, they knew they would be indicted for treason. On the other hand, the Revolution itself was, for the time being, uncontrollable.

All their elaborate theories about constitutional government
had become irrelevant, and they were caught between two
fires.

Nevertheless, the mobs of soldiers and factory workers
who flocked to the Tauride Palace, the seat of the Duma,
were looking for bourgeois guidance in the extremity that
had occurred. The Duma, as such, failed to rise to the occasion. The last act of the Imperial Cabinet, before its members slunk away into hiding on the night of 27 February,
had been to issue an edict, signed beforehand by the Tsar,
proroguing the Duma. It was here that one might have
expected history to repeat itself, and the Duma to follow the
example of the Third Estate of the French States-General in
1789, swearing a new Oath of the Tennis Court and refusing
to disperse. But the fourth Duma, elected on a restricted
franchise, was in spirit far less revolutionary than the French
Commons, chosen by universal suffrage. Its anti-government
oratory had been aimed at limited targets: the inefficient
conduct of the war, the evil influence of Rasputin, or the
alleged pro-German sympathies of the Empress. Its liberal
leaders had desired a palace revolution, from which they
fondly imagined that the great benefits of constitutional and
social reform would proceed in an orderly manner. They
had no immediate plans for turning everything upside down,
with the result that they were unprepared to lead a corporate
parliamentary effort to take charge of a dangerous situation.
After the Tsar's decree of prorogation had been promulgated
the Duma never formally met. Its members held a 'private'
meeting, not in the accustomed Hall of Plenary Session, but
in an adjoining chamber, from which members of the right-
wing parties absented themselves. Those present entrusted
the formation of an emergency committee 'for the re-
establishment of order in the capital and for contacts with
persons and institutions' to the unofficial steering committee of party leaders; out of this, a few days later, the
Provisional Government was formed.

'Contact with persons and institutions.' This phrase
betrayed the helplessness of the unrepresentative bourgeois
parliament upon which destiny had placed the decision of
the hour. Who were those persons, and what were those

institutions, available to fill the void left by the departed regime?

Throughout all the excesses of the French Revolution the thread of legitimacy stemming from the power originally conceded by the King to the States-General, which turned itself into the National Assembly, was never formally broken. In the Russian Revolution no thread of legitimacy was ever established. The Tsar's abdication was itself unconstitutional, for he had no right to pass over his son in favour of his brother Michael. But at least he thought he was acting in association with the Imperial Duma, and the generals who advised him to abdicate thought that order had been restored in the capital under a government of constitutional monarchists responsible to that Duma. But Michael, when he in turn abdicated, was already aware that the Revolution had gone much further. The new ministers failed to reinsure their position by obtaining a formal vote of confidence from the Duma. They thereby deprived themselves of the authority that alone would have attracted the loyalty of those elements in the State machine who might have rallied the forces of law and order. As an acute French observer, the Comte de Chambrun, remarked at the time, 'the wheel turns, but here Gracchus Baboeuf appears on the second day. The Revolution is jumping some of its stages.' It was to jump more of them when Lenin arrived. Milyukov, leader of the Cadet Party, presented the new government to the crowd in the Duma chamber, and when he was asked by hostile voices 'Who chose you?' he could only reply, against all his inclinations, and amid jeers, 'We have been elected by the Revolution.'

Liberal democracy thus went by default. Revolutionary democracy, and at that time it was a genuine democracy, rushed in to fill the gap. The Executive Committee (Excom) of the Petrograd Soviet was originally composed of minor revolutionaries who happened to be in the capital at the unexpected moment, and not in gaol or exile. But as the Revolution spread throughout the country and the dormant machinery of workers' soviets dating from 1905 reactivated itself, as political prisoners were released and exiles returned, the Executive Committee achieved, through elections in factories and regiments, a truly democratic base. If there can be such a thing as revolutionary legitimacy the Soviet possessed it, but the Cadet leader Milyukov and his well-heeled friends did not.

All the same, by Friday, 3 March, Russia had a government of sorts, headed by a prince and composed of wealthy and solid members of the bourgeoisie. Kerensky, as Minister of Justice, was the only socialist among them. He had a foot in both camps, and it was he who had negotiated a working agreement with the Petrograd Soviet by which the Provisional Government, with the Excom's consent, was to rule until such time as a Constituent Assembly could be elected by universal suffrage.

Rodzianko, President of the Duma, who by reason of his office had taken a leading part in negotiating the abdication, was not, after all, a member of the new ministry. He was an Octobrist, a member of the party of liberal landlords, but this was the hour of the Cadets, the party of the liberal bourgeoisie. So Prince Lvov, the senior head of the Voluntary Organizations, was borne up on the tide of history to become the nominal head of the government that had supplanted the Tsar. The real leader was the Foreign Minister, Milyukov, chairman and founder of the party, who was at least a serious politician. Guchkov became Minister of War, and Tereshchenko, a sugar millionaire and reputed to be the richest man in Russia, took the portfolio of Finance.

All these frock-coated gentlemen knew one another well, having met frequently not only in the corridors of the Duma but on the boards of the various Volunteer Organizations and in clubs and salons. Indeed, having wrested from the bureaucracy the major responsibility for the civilian side of the war effort, they had come to regard themselves, long before the Revolution, as the effective government of Russia. It now remained to be seen whether, having assumed the full trappings of authority, they could deal with the Soviet as effectively as they had dealt with the Tsar.

They suffered their first defeat at the very outset. Most of them would have liked a constitutional monarchy, but they soon found that, in the revolutionary temper of the time, this was totally out of the question. As they assumed office a red flag flew over the Winter Palace and the imperial emblems were being removed wherever they were found. Russia, though not yet officially a republic, was certainly no longer a monarchy. The lynch-pin of the Empire had been withdrawn, and no one knew yet what was going to be put in its place.

The surprising thing was the ease with which the old crowned order, with all its appurtenances of imperial grandeur, vanished into thin air. The Emperor had returned as a prisoner to his family in their palace at Tsarskoye Selo, whence nearly all their courtiers had fled and where most of their friends left them severely alone.

'One of the most characteristic features of the Revolution,' wrote Paléologue in his journal at the time, 'is the immediate and total void created round the threatened sovereigns. The moment collisions with the mob took place all the regiments of the Guard, including the magnificent Cossacks of the Escort, betrayed their oath of fealty. Nor has a single grand duke risen to defend the sacred person of the monarch; one of them actually placed his unit at the service of the rebels even before the Emperor's abdication. In fact, with a few exceptions which are all the more creditable, there has been wholesale desertion on the part of the Court crowd and all those *pridvorny*, high officers and dignitaries who, amid the pomp and pageantry of ceremonies and processions, seemed to be the natural guardians of the throne.'[2]

On 1 March, the palace garrison of Tsarskoye Selo itself made its appearance at the Duma.

'At the head were the Cossacks of the Escort, those magnificent horsemen who are the flower of the *Kasatchevo*, the proud and privileged élite of the Imperial Guard. Then came the Regiment of His Majesty, the Sacred Legion recruited by selection from all the units of the Guard and whose special function it is to secure the personal safety of their sovereigns. Next came His Majesty's Railway Regiment which has the duty of conducting the imperial trains and watching over the safety of Their Majesties when travelling. At the end of the procession marched the Police of the Imperial Palaces, chosen satellites who have to guard the imperial residences from within and thus participate daily in the intimate private life of their masters. All of these men, officers and privates alike, have vowed their devotion to the new authority – whose very name they do not know – as if they could not embrace the chains of a new servitude too soon. My mind went back to the brave Swiss, who let themselves be cut to pieces on the steps of the Tuileries on 10 August 1792, though Louis XVI was not their sovereign.'³

A very few stayed faithful to the end: Count Beckendorff, the Court Chamberlain, and his wife; Count Zamoisky, who walked all the way to Tsarskoye Selo to offer his services to the Tsaritsa; Bunting, Governor of Tver, who later committed suicide; and Bark, the Food Minister, who was offered a portfolio in the new administration, but declined 'on principle'.

The Emperor's detention in his palace began on 8 March. Out of all his glittering Court, he and his family were attended by six ladies and five gentlemen, one of whom discreetly left four days later. Nicholas was right to have written in his diary: 'All around me I see treason, cowardice and deceit.'

Perhaps Sukhanov was right to describe him as 'the musical comedy sovereign of a sixth of the globe'.

About this time Paléologue dined privately with a dozen persons who had all been very well-known figures at Court. 'At table the conversations à deux very quickly petered out, and a general discussion on the subject of Nicholas II began. In spite of his present misery and the terrifying prospects of his immediate future, the company passed the severest judgements on all the acts of his reign; he was overwhelmed with a torrent of reproach for old and recent grievances.'⁴

Paléologue's dinner companions were relatively minor figures, as yet unmolested. The immediate victims of the Revolution were those who could be identified with the actual control of the fallen regime – ministers, police chiefs, some of the provincial governors, Rasputin's creatures among the higher clergy, and, inevitably, the talented and beautiful but over-ostentatious *prima ballerina assoluta* Kschessinska, the Madame du Barry of this revolution. Such personages either went into hiding or were arrested, and most of them had their splendid houses looted.

The hated turncoat Protopopov, who, as the Tsar's last Minister of the Interior, was the final legitimate departmental authority to confront the riotous situation in the streets, was persuaded to resign on the fateful Monday by his frightened colleagues, who were still hoping that, by sacrificing this butt of the liberals, they might save themselves. Without the approval of the Tsar such a resignation could not take formal effect, but Protopopov, true to the end to his tragi-comical role as a kind of reincarnation of Rasputin, staggered out of the last Cabinet meeting threatening suicide. In fact, he took refuge in the shop of his tailor, and next day surrendered to the Duma, where he was duly arrested.

The squalor of the end of the mighty Tsarist regime is one of the cruellest ironies of history. The Emperor meekly abdicating in a railway siding at the behest of his favourite generals, the deserted Empress in her palace watching at the bedside of her children stricken with measles, ministers hurrying away from an isolated seat of government to lose themselves in the crowd – these were the appearances that marked the close of three proud centuries of Romanov rule. The vast paraphernalia of courtiers, governors, noblemen and generals that had been sustained by that rule failed, at the last, to rally round it.

Nevertheless, it was not yet the turn of the propertied classes, as such, to resign their wealth and influence. Certain tall poppies fell first to the reaper – symbolic sacrifices on the revolutionary altar. Typical of these was Countess Kleinmichel, a meddlesome septuagenarian of the higher aristocracy who, although of no great political importance, had contrived to make an enemy of Rodzianko. On that Monday night when the Tsarist regime finally collapsed, she had invited a few titled friends to dine with her. Just as her old butler, Andrei, threw open the folding-doors and announced that dinner was served, there was a great commotion as servants rushed in to cry that armed men had broken in by the back door. Lieutenant Baron de Pilar, one of the guests, seized his sword to repel the invaders, but the Countess urged escape by the grand staircase. The company took refuge in the house of the Baron's father, on the opposite side of the street, whence the Countess had the mortification of watching the soldiers and sailors dragging her beautiful ballroom furniture about and being served with food and wine by her own butler.

Next day the Countess found sanctuary in the Chinese Legation, but on the third evening about fifteen soldiers broke into it, saying they had come to arrest her. The Chinese Minister protested at this breach of diplomatic immunity, and telephoned Sir George Buchanan, the British Ambassador, to ask him to use his influence on behalf of the lady who had taken shelter with him. According to the Countess, the Ambassador replied that he, like the French and Italian heads of mission, had promised not to meddle in Russia's internal affairs, and had renounced their right to shelter fugitives. To save the Chinese and their children from molestation, the Countess agreed to follow the soldiers to the Duma, where she was placed under arrest as 'an enemy of the people'.

'Motorcars kept arriving', she wrote afterwards, 'bringing Ministers, courtiers and generals who had been arrested. The vast rooms of the Tauride Palace, where Potemkin the Magnificent had given so many fêtes for the Northern Semiramis [Catherine the Great], witnessed anew, and for the last time, a gathering of all the distinguished people of the metropolis: aristocrats, society people and high civilian and military officers.

'I was sitting at a table with some kindly members of the Duma, who had offered me a cup of tea, when a general who had been arrested collapsed into a chair near me and said with emotion: "Madam, you and I are present at the fall of a great empire." '[5]

The same scene was observed by Lieutenant Aleksei Tarasov-Rodianov, a member of the machine gun regiment stationed at Oranienbaum, who had been a secret Bolshevik. 'Good Lord!' he wrote, 'what a change has taken place in these Tsarist dignitaries! An ordinary light coat over a bowed back, a torn scarf, dirty shoes. How different from the haughty, gold-braided uniforms, the brocade-striped white trousers, the jaunty plumes of cocked hats!'[6]

Sukhanov noticed these same dignitaries standing against a wall in a tight little bunch and surrounded by armed men.

'A crowd of soldiers in a rather aggressive mood pressed round them, flinging out hostile remarks. Kurlov looked very grim. He was pale but seemed in possession of himself; he was looking round and listening to the remarks, half challengingly. On the other hand Stuermer, in utter panic and confusion, with a hangdog look and chattering teeth, made an extremely disagreeable impression.'[7]

Others of the old regime who came into the hall, not under arrest, had a different air, according to Tarasov-Rodianov. 'They were very formal, and the gleam of their polished boots and pomaded hair belied the mortal terror of their souls. They smoked their cigarettes with studied negligence, stood in stiff, solemn postures, and stole covert, cowardly glances at the soldiers. Officials of various magistracies were fawning around, procuring orders to protect their dwellings against search-warrants.'[8]

Next morning Countess Kleinmichel was awakened by the powerful voice of a colonel of the General Staff reading the manifesto announcing the abdication of Nicholas II.

'I swallowed a cup of tea, and, having observed the joy of shorthand-typists, nurses, students and officers, who were all embracing with the same mad frenzy, I left the room, for I saw that my saddened mood angered them. The first thing I noticed in the passage was the numerous officers of the Tsar's escort, Caucasian Cossacks, whose fidelity and devotion I had praised all my life. These officers were not content with red bows; they had put large scarlet scarves across their breasts, from shoulder to waist. They were surrounded by deputies who shook them by the hand, congratulated them and thanked them for their decision.'[9]

Three days later the Countess was released. Making her way home on foot she found her house partly looted and partly destroyed. It had been turned into quarters for soldiers who had lost touch with their regiments, and had become, in fact, a vast hostel where male and female students prepared meals not only in the kitchens but in the reception rooms, sang revolutionary songs, made speeches to the soldiers and in the evening danced madly to the sound of the piano. 'I was immediately compelled to associate myself with such hospitality by a gift of 5,000 roubles. I had been left the use of two rooms for myself and seven or eight for my servants.'[10]

The grand dukes who happened to be in the capital escaped the immediate vengeance of the Revolution. As a fifth wheel of the imperial coach, most of them were virtually unknown to the general public, whether of the bourgeoisie or the working class. Some of them had lent an ear to the futile last-minute plots in Court circles to depose the Tsar, but only two of them had a role to play in the real-life drama. One was Michael, the Tsar's brother, who technically succeeded to the Throne after Nicholas's abdication, but ingloriously renounced it next day when he saw the way the wind was blowing. The other was Cyril, who, sporting a red rosette, marched at the head of his naval regiment to submit to the Duma, even before the abdication was a legal fact. The rest of the family slipped into temporary obscurity. Only the Grand Duke Paul remained near the Empress, as she waited at Tsarskoye Selo for the return of the captive Emperor. The Romanov clan, the most privileged in Europe, disintegrated at the first sound of gunfire.

Their most faithful servant, however, felt the immediate force of the blast. The octogenarian Count Fredericks had occupied the key post of Minister of the Imperial Court for two decades. Though technically a member of the Government, he had never attended a Cabinet meeting, and had occupied himself solely with matters of Court protocol and the personal affairs of the imperial family. He was, in fact, the one stable figure in the dissolving Court scene, resisting, as far as lay within his power, the malign influence of Rasputin, offering sound advice to his sovereign on ceremonial matters and acting as an understanding Dutch uncle to the wayward grand dukes.

This excellent personification of what was best in the fallen regime was arrested while in attendance on the Tsar at Headquarters and, since he was suffering from a disease of the bladder, was lodged in the French Hospital in Petrograd. He complained, when examined by the Muravyev Commission set up by the Provisional Government to investigate alleged breaches of the old law by the highest officers of the Tsarist regime, that at least two soldiers with fixed bayonets guarded him night and day, and refused him the most elementary privacy. They addressed him with the familiar 'thou', which deeply offended his sense of military propriety, and no provision was made for him to see his ailing wife.

The Countess, aged 82, was in bed with pneumonia when soldiers from her husband's own regiment, the Horse Guards, broke into their house and looted it. A servant wrapped her in blankets and took her to the neighbouring flat of Princess Belosselsky, the wife of the Horse Guards colonel, but this lady, bedridden herself, dared not receive her. Helped by her daughter Emma she managed to reach the English Hospital, but, according to Countess Kleinmichel, the British Ambassador had forbidden the doctor in charge to admit anyone associated with the fallen regime. Countess Fredericks was again turned out into the streets, in twenty degrees of frost, and eventually found refuge in the humble flat of her Italian music master. 'In vain', wrote Countess Kleinmichel, 'did Emma try to find another place of shelter for her mother; nobody would have them; their friends and acquaintances pretended they did not know them.'[11] The Countess died shortly afterwards, in an isolation hospital; her husband, once the supreme dictator of the Court who granted favours to a thousand suppliants, was later released, and, for a little while yet, was to be seen walking alone along the Nevsky Prospect in his faded Court uniform, until the' Bolsheviks allowed him to go to Finland, where he died at the age of 84.

The top policemen stayed in their homes while their colleagues were being chased and slaughtered. They had had their ears to the ground, and were in a better position than most to distinguish between a revolt and a revolution. The local head of the Okhrana, the dreaded secret police, had prudently furnished himself with foreign money and a false passport. He fled from house to house, and at an early opportunity slipped away southwards, eventually leaving Russia altogether, to turn up as a porter at the Gare du Nord, Paris.

Kschessinska was clearly destined to be an object of mob revenge. Her last public appearance had been on the imperial stage of the Mariinsky Theatre, where she had been dancing for twenty-seven years. It was a charity performance under the patronage of the Empress, in which she danced with Fokine in his ballet *Carnaval* before 'a very elegant and select audience'. Already a menacing atmosphere hung over the capital, and a day or so later General Halle, chief of police for her district, at a time when the Tsar's own ministers were still showing every sign of complacency, warned her that in her pretentious palace on the Kamenno-Ostrovsky Prospect she was peculiarly vulnerable and suggested she should leave Petrograd for a time. Her grand ducal lover Andrei was taking a cure at Kislovodsk, on leave from his nominal military duties, so she left with their young son and the male ballet dancer Vladimirov for the safety of a Finnish spa. But when the fears of the police seemed unjustified she returned to the capital and, to celebrate, decided to give what was to prove the last of her great dinner parties. There were twenty-four covers, and, with typical vulgarity, she brought out all her precious trinkets and works of art, stored since the beginning of the war, until there was no room left to display them. Among them were 'a superb collection of artificial flowers made of precious stones and a small gold firtree, its branches shimmering with little diamonds'.[12]

Next day, the 23rd, while her housekeeper was wisely checking the silver, glass and linen, her small son ran in to tell her that a huge crowd was pouring out of Great Dvorianskaya Street. But for the next three days, she records in her book, she had no thought of revolution. On the Saturday 'I went quite normally to the Alexander Theatre where Yuriev's 25th stage anniversary was being celebrated with Lermontov's *Masquerade,* produced by Meierhold. The audience was tense and nervous. There was the sound of firing from some quarters, but I was able to return without trouble.'[13]

On the following day the dancer's police admirer telephoned her repeatedly to say the situation was very serious, although he still hoped it might improve if 'the abscess burst'. He advised her to save what she could from her palace. 'Although I never kept my large diamonds and jewellery at home but left it with Fabergé, I still had at home a great number of small jewels, not to mention the silver and other precious objects with which my rooms were decorated. What was I to choose? What was I to take away, and where? In the street the storm was already raging.'[14]

Kschessinska decided to put her most valuable possessions in a suitcase and await events. The abscess did not burst, at least not in the way General Halle had hoped. On the fateful Monday there was distant firing all day, and at dinnertime there were explosions not far from the palace. Wearing a shawl, her little fox-terrier Djibi under her arm, and accompanied by her son and a handful of friends, she fled on foot to Yuriev's flat. The troops who kept bursting in, looking in vain for police machine guns on the roof, did not recognize her. For three days she did not dare to undress, and slept in the passage to avoid stray bullets.

The palace on the Kamenno-Ostrovsky Prospect was occupied on the night she fled by a gang led by a Georgian student named Agabagov. She learned that her house-keeper, a widow whom she had befriended, welcomed them with open arms, crying 'Come in, come in! The bird has flown.' Agabagov gave a great many dinner parties, forcing her cook to serve him and his guests. Her two cars were requisitioned. A few days later the palace was looted by the mob. Paléologue, who happened to observe the scene and recalled the more than diplomatic privileges that the ballerina had enjoyed, uttered the cryptic remark: 'A revolution is always more or less a summary and a sanction.'[15] The sanction was confirmed later when the dainty palace became the first headquarters of Lenin and his Bolsheviks, whom the Provisional Government proved powerless to evict.

To innocent children of the aristocracy the events of those first revolutionary days were even more inexplicable. Princess Zinaida Shakhovskoi was ten years old and a pupil at St Catherine's, one of Petrograd's 'institutes', or imperial boarding schools for daughters of the nobility.

Sundays were visiting days for parents, but on 26 February the throng in the large white-columned hall was noticeably thinner than usual. After Zinaida and her elder sister had taken leave of their mother the colonnaded palace, which Peter the Great built for his sister Natalya, soon became 'the scene of unfamiliar agitation; visibly bewildered, our "lady teachers" paid us the least possible attention. The chamber-maids and the bearded and medallioned ushers brought mattresses into our classroom, where we were to spend the night because it fronted on to an interior garden and some-thing strange was happening in the streets of the town. The long corridors, usually so silent, were filled with the clatter of the Emperor's pages, a detachment of whom had arrived to protect us from a danger of which we knew nothing. All of us, from the girls in my own class to the sixth-formers in their mauve dresses, were terribly excited by the boys' presence. As a rule, only brothers and cousins were allowed into the seminary, and they were subject to the strict supervision of visitors' days.

'I had no sense of discipline. I left the others and crept into the hall, dominated by the portraits of two Empresses. Its windows looked out on to Fontanka river. I could see nothing; the curtains were drawn and mattresses placed against the panes. For the first time I heard the sound which was soon to become so familiar, the sound of machine-gun fire. The revolution of February 1917 had made itself known to me. I did not know the meaning of the word "revolution". That day I associated it with disorder.'[16]

During the next few days, in this unreal atmosphere, where over their tight corsets the girls wore long dresses that would have suited the court ladies of Catherine the Great, everyone awaited the vague and inaccurate items of news that filtered through from the outside world.

'One evening we were all of us – greens, reds and mauves – assembled for prayers, and the mistress who led them omitted the customary prayer for the Tsar. The older girls, like the "lady teachers", dabbed at their eyes with handker-chiefs; one caught the sound of sobbing, and suddenly realized that something very grave had happened to Russia and to us all.'[17]

The next day some of the mothers came to take their daughters away. Catherine's Institute was seeing its last days.

They were the last days of much else. The Russian Empire had been a police state contained within a military carapace. Suddenly it had ceased to be so, and, though its capitalist economy was still more or less intact, that economy was now naked and unprotected. Businessmen might still be making profits, but in a world from which the traditional guarantees of order had disappeared.

Officers were having to register with an organization established in their own Army and Navy Club, appearing before a committee composed of students and private soldiers sitting at a big table, towards which they were roughly pushed by the crowd of soldiers filling the room.

From that time onwards many people, who had never experienced it or imagined it could happen to them, were roughly pushed. As for discomfort, it was soon to be the lot of all, but it came quickest to gentlefolk who lived in straitened circumstances. The writer E. M. Almedingen, who with her English mother occupied a modest apartment in a big block in Mochovaya Street, watched at night the police station opposite going up in flames.

'There were no firemen anywhere; the building was meant to burn, and burn it did. Few people, if any, went to bed that night.

'Next morning there was no water to be had in our whole vast building, and never again in Russia was I to see water running from a tap in any house I lived in.'[18]

The biggest discomfort, and the eeriest, for all well-nurtured people, was the sudden realization that their position in the scheme of things was no longer automatically protected by the old conventions of class behaviour. In 1905 there had been a national revolt against the Autocracy, in which many privileged individuals suffered; but the social fabric itself had not been threatened. Since then the under-lying violence of Russian life had broken surface here and there, in strikes, demonstrations and *jacqueries*; but these were exceptions that proved the rule, and the rule was that of a social order instinctively obeyed by most of the people most of the time. One might be robbed in full daylight in the streets of Petrograd, but the policeman would be sympathetic.

Now this inner stability of the propertied classes had gone, never to be re-established. Many appearances had not changed, but the reality had. Each man was on his own, with his personal fears, hopes, joys, and ambitions, and he had to relate himself to the Revolution as an individual and not as a member of a class.

Everyone who had been accustomed to exercise authority, whether as administrator, employer, manager or even head of a well-staffed household, now felt himself to be under the surveillance of those beneath him. A hierarchy that a few days before had been absolute had become conditional. This applied no less to affairs of State than to the conduct of a factory. When members of the Provisional Government went to inspect the troops at the front they were well aware that they would not have found seats in the train without the approval of the Petrograd Soviet. A witty observer remarked: 'The old government is in prison, and the new one is under house arrest.'

Sir Robert Bruce Lockhart wrote in his report to the British Ambassador: 'It seems impossible that the dispute between the bourgeoisie and the proletariat can be liquidated without further bloodshed. When this clash will come no one knows.'[19]

5

'In That Dawn'

On 5 March, the first Sunday of the Revolution, Marylie Markovitch, a Frenchwoman who had married into the Russian nobility, ventured again into the streets of Petrograd. 'The crisis is over,' she wrote, 'at least in its acute phase. No more shouts, no more shots. We are waking up – from a nightmare or from a dream?'[1]

The weather had changed, and there was the freshness of spring in the air. Normal life had been resumed. Housewives, baskets on their arms, awaited their turn at the food shops. 'Bread was available at last – the bread of the Revolution!' Well-dressed people were seen abroad again. Errand boys drew their familiar sledges across the melting snow; office workers were taking the air, ready to return to their jobs next day. From a neighbouring Guards barracks, a military band played the *Marseillaise*, to the applause of the crowd. Strangers embraced. It was the honeymoon of the Revolution.

A Russian friend accosted Madame Markovitch. 'With us it is not as in France; we have made our Revolution with almost no bloodshed.'

A more considerate stroller intervened: 'But of course the French Revolution happened over a century ago. People are more civilized today.'[2]

The French Ambassador, with many problems on his

mind, was also out that Sunday. After assisting at his Latin Mass in the embassy chapel he dropped in at three crowded churches, including the Preobrajensky Cathedral. A week before it had been well-nigh impossible to dissociate the Russian Orthodox Church from its earthly protector the Tsar, but now the frequent prayers in the Liturgy for him, his Empress, the heir to the throne and all the imperial family had been abolished by order of the Holy Synod, and nothing as yet had taken their place.

'The same scene met me everywhere; a grave and silent congregation exchanging amazed and melancholy glances. Some of the mujiks looked bewildered and horrified, and several had tears in their eyes. Yet even among those who seemed the most moved I could not find one who did not sport a red cockade or armband.'[3]

The red cockades survived this first mood of peasant bewilderment. There were few in Russia at that time who did not expect something good to come out of their release from the Tsarist straitjacket. Outside the immediate circles of the fallen Court and Government, and of those serving officers and policemen shaken by having watched their colleagues butchered, the way seemed open to a variety of bright futures. 'Bliss was it in that dawn to be alive.' Liberal democracy, socialist idealism, academic freedom, a rebirth of the arts, even new commercial opportunities – such competing dreams filled many minds before the true pattern of the future began to take shape.

Sukhanov, who had been the chief Soviet figure in the negotiations that had produced the Provisional Government, writing perhaps with the benefit of hindsight, claimed that he and his friends looked beyond this middle-class euphoria. 'Newspapers appeared. The whole of the old bourgeois and yellow press burst out with a deafening noise on the horns and kettle-drums; during those days they poured out a whole sea of enthusiasm, emotion and benevolence. People who had had no more to do with the Revolution than with last year's snows, and who regarded the working class as at best a nagging creditor, now overflowed with love of liberty, devotion to the Constituent Assembly and compliments on the heroism and good sense of the masses of the people and their leaders. In the Excom we looked through the bulky numbers and the rapturous leading articles of the newspapers with the condescending smile of victors.'[4]

Nevertheless, though the Court was no more, great wealth still existed, if on unsure foundations, and the Petrograd *demi-monde* came into its own again. One by one the smart restaurants re-opened, welcoming much the same group of wartime profiteers. The solid rich were adjusting themselves to new values, of the true nature of which they were as yet uncertain. Perforce embracing the Revolution, they hoped that, though they now had to 'meet the people' in various unheard-of ways, they would be able to reconstitute their old lives amid all this ferment of impassioned street oratory and social upheaval.

Euphoria there certainly was, among all classes. A starry-eyed English journalist felt able to write: 'Never was any country in the world as interesting as Russia now is. Old men are saying "Nunc dimittis"; young men are singing in the dawn; and I have met many men and women who seem walking in a hushed sense of benediction.'

Meanwhile, as well as singing in the dawn, people were beginning to ask themselves a number of urgent questions. The basic one was: who was to rule the new Russia? Was it to be the workers and soldiers who had actually accomplished the Revolution, or the men of the Duma who had, in a somewhat muddled way, accepted it? On this hung the question of the extent of the Revolution. Was it to be limited to the establishment of constitutional government, on the British or the French model, or was it to lead to the transformation of society for which the various groups of socialists indubitably stood?

But first, was there to be a new Russia at all, outside Petrograd? The fall of the Autocracy had been brought about in a single town, which contained less than 1·4 per cent of the population of the Empire. Could those brief days of street fighting, in an area of a few square miles at the extreme edge of the vast land-mass, determine the fate of all the rest?

This question was soon answered. The key to it was the abdication of the Tsar. Once the collapse of his all-embracing authority was known, every Russian, high or low, was confronted with the problem of its replacement.

The news from Petrograd was carried everywhere, first by telegraph, and then by travellers on the railway. These were the two chief means of communication in the Russia of 1917, which had few serviceable roads, and in wartime their operation was necessarily unpredictable. Thus the people of Pskov, where the Tsar in fact abdicated, learned of the full extent of the Revolution a fortnight later than did those of Nikolaevsk, by the Black Sea. In Mogilev, where army headquarters were established, nothing conclusive was known until the middle of March. But in Moscow, the sister capital, the overturn was completed peacefully a day or two after the Petrograd events.

Everywhere the pattern was much the same. The top Tsarist officials and the police were the first to abandon their posts, for the most part voluntarily, and the local municipalities and county councils assumed what authority they could muster. Simultaneously, the district soviets of workers and peasants, which had carried on an underground existence since 1905, came into the open and, in the name of freedom, entered into what seemed at first like fraternal relations with the liberated bourgeoisie.

It was evident from the start that the Provisional Government had no means of controlling this situation. It did not dispose of enough personnel to take proper charge of the now headless Tsarist administrative machine, whether in Petrograd or in the outlying regions. Its first act was to accept the situation as it found it, and dismiss by telegraph all provincial and town governors. In their place it attempted to nominate the existing bourgeois mayors and the noblemen who chaired the zemstvos. But, pending the arrival in various parts of the country of the officials to whom the Government gave the ominous name of 'commissar', the real local administration was to a large extent assumed by those who alone were capable of preserving some semblance of law and order – the newly emergent soviets.

Konstantin Paustovsky described Dr Kishkin, the commissar sent to Moscow, as 'a dry stick of a man, with a greying beard and the eyes of a martyr, who went about in an elegant frock coat with silk lapels and wore a red rose in his buttonhole. It never entered anybody's head to carry out his orders.'[5]

By 4 March Prince Lvov was already beginning to despair of the situation. According to Kerensky he threw a bundle of telegrams on the Cabinet table and said:

'Look what is happening, gentlemen. Since yesterday telegrams like these have been pouring in from all parts of European Russia. These are no longer the messages of support you have all been reading. These are official reports from all the provincial capitals and from many smaller towns. They all say more or less the same thing: that at the first news of the fall of the monarchy the local administration has fled, beginning with the governor and ending with the lowliest policeman, and those higher officials, particularly in the police, who either would not or could not get away in time have been arrested by all kinds of self-appointed revolutionary authorities and public committees.'

'There was dead silence in the room,' wrote Kerensky, 'as each of us wondered what to do. Here we were in the middle of a war, and large areas of the country had passed into the hands of completely unknown people!'[6]

This was probably an exaggeration. The bourgeoisie were represented in most of the new town 'coalitions', and in the countryside, where the landowners were still in their mansions, the rural hierarchy was threatened rather than disturbed. The demand for full worker participation in the factories and for an eight-hour day, like the demand for the carving up of private estates, took some time to formulate. Everyone was waiting for a lead from Petrograd, which, in the confusion of the hour, was slow in coming.

The habit of waiting for orders from the centre was so engrained in the bourgeoisie that only in a few towns did they take a positive initiative, and it usually failed. This happened in Nizhny-Novgorod, the great fair centre on the Volga where Gorky had met his self-made millionaire. There, according to Dumaev, a local working-class leader, the old municipality wanted to organize a Committee for the Re-establishment of Order which would co-opt only acceptable workers. But, presenting themselves as delegates of the town soviet, a group of workers demanded the arrest of the governor and the release of political prisoners. A few days later the soviet effected this themselves. The bourgeoisie then wanted to replace the governor with the chairman of the district zemstvo, but the soviet insisted on an executive committee instead, which was formed of three bourgeois, three workers and a soldiers' representative.

More typical was Baku, the oil town in Azerbaijan on the Caspian Sea, noted politically as the cradle of the 1905 near-revolution. Baku was dominated by Russia's oil kings, who lived in great style in mansions on the shore. The ballerina Kschessinska, who had danced there a few weeks before the Revolution, had remarked on the elegance of her audience.

When the news of the Tsar's abdication reached the town on 3 March, there was rejoicing among all classes. Only Admiral Kliupfel, commandant of the marine garrison, and two particularly unpopular police officers were arrested. The theatres continued to play to capacity audiences, who stood for the playing of the *Marseillaise*.

When the city duma met in the town hall, representatives of the trade unions and co-operatives assembled in an upstairs room to form a soviet. The Stock Exchange Committee and the Council of Oil Industries were against the appointment of an executive committee representing both the duma and the soviet, but the majority of the duma agreed to it. The mayor, L. L. Bych, formally inaugurated the committee, the leadership of which fell to 'public men' of liberal sympathies. A Cadet lawyer became head of the municipal police, and a Bolshevik named Stopani, because of his wartime experience in the co-operatives, was appointed assistant chairman and head of the supply committee. Meanwhile the Provisional Government had entrusted the administration of the whole of Transcaucasia to a body headed by the Cadet V. A. Kharlamov. There were no zemstvos in this outlying part of the Empire.

On 6 March, a local Bolshevik hero, Shaumian, who had distinguished himself in the Baku strike of 1914, returned in triumph from Siberian exile. He was made chairman of the soviet, even though it contained only nine Bolsheviks out of the fifty-two delegates. He was also elected to the executive committee, and, in the spirit of the hour, was warmly welcomed to it by the bourgeois mayor Bych.

This was a microcosm of what was happening in Petrograd itself, where the cultured members of the Imperial Duma, upon whom the mantle of State had so unexpectedly fallen, were having to share their splendid and solemn meeting-place with the odd assortment of characters who were drifting together to form the central Soviet.

'On the first day,' wrote Prince Mansyrev, 'the revolutionaries occupied only one room of the Tauride Palace, then one or two others. Then they occupied the restaurant, the post office, the left wing of the building, the chancery, the President's office. Soon there were only the library and the administrative office remaining. Farewell, Duma!'

The Tauride Palace was described at this time as looking like an immense guardroom.

'Soldiers are everywhere,' wrote Robien, 'all unbuttoned and eating at dirty wooden tables or sprawling on the floor round a samovar. Others, still carrying arms, are asleep on top of piled-up sacks of flour, brought there as food supplies for the town, which cover everything with white dust. The floor is filthy, littered with bits of paper, cigarette ends and rubbish of all kinds. Unshaven students with long mops of hair, wearing green caps, and girl typists with short hair and pince-nez glasses – typical Russian Nihilists – move about among the soldiers. It makes a lamentable impression in this Empire interior with its classical columns. The portrait of the Emperor has been removed.'[7]

On 11 (25) March the ambassadors of Britain, France and Italy, anxious to keep Russia in the war, went in full diplomatic dress to the Mariinsky Palace to give official recognition to the Provisional Government. Paléologue noted:

'The appearance of the beautiful building, which was once presented by Nicholas I to his favourite daughter the Duchess of Leuchtenburg, and afterwards became the seat of the Council of Empire, had already changed. In the vestibule, where the lackeys, resplendent in their Court livery, used to be in attendance, unkempt, unwashed soldiers were sprawling over the seats, smoking with an insolent leer. The great marble staircases had not been swept since the Revolution. No one was there to receive us, though what we were about to perform was an act of state. Then and there I could not help thinking of a ceremony "in the august presence of His Majesty the Emperor". How perfect the arrangements! What pomp and pageantry! What a turn-out of the official hierarchy! If Baron Korff, Grand Master of Ceremonies, could have seen us at that moment he would have fainted with shame.

'Milyukov, the new Foreign Minister, came forward; he took us to one room, then another, then a third, not knowing where to stop and groping for a switch to turn on the light. "Here we are at last. I think this will suit us all right." He went off to find his colleagues, who came at once. They were all in working dress, carrying their portfolios under their arms.'[8]

This physical disarray was matched everywhere by intellectual confusion. A few weeks before the collapse of the Autocracy, Konstantin Paustovsky, as a young journalist, had been sent by his Moscow newspaper to a nearby provincial town to report on the political situation in the countryside. He recorded how, when the great news came, the first reaction among people of all classes was to rush to the local printer's to get the Provisional Government's proclamation printed. As the tidings spread by word of mouth peasants arrived hot-foot to inquire what was to happen to the gentry's land; while self-appointed orators appeared on the streets, offering every kind of nostrum for the well-being of a brave new world.

Yet the substance of Russian society had not yet undergone any radical transformation. Its political skin had been flayed, and no one knew with what it would be replaced. After the initial violence had died down, all but a handful of the members of the ruling classes were left in possession of what they considered to be theirs by right. Industrialists got their factories going again, the stock exchanges and private banks resumed their function, most of the exclusive clubs re-opened, and country squires, pending the new agrarian reform which clearly loomed ahead, stayed quietly on their estates.

It could not be denied, however, that change was in the air, and that relationships between the haves and the have-nots had already undergone a palpable alteration. Factory managers soon found themselves on the defensive in their dealings with the nascent work committees and no landed gentleman felt himself to be complete master of his estates when their fate was to be decided by the coming Constituent Assembly and when he had to deal with the mixed local comittee established to ensure the free supply of grain. Domestic servants threw off their ancient servility; in Petrograd, in the second week of the Revolution, they were all bidden by the Soviet to assemble in the nearest cinema, where old retainers formulated demands for an eight-hour day, the doubling of their wages and the run of their mistresses' apartments on one day a month for the entertainment of their own friends.

A twelve or ten-hour day, six days a week, had long been the lot of most of Russia's industrial workers, and that this should be reduced to an eight-hour day had been their traditional social demand ever since 1905. Suddenly, on 10 March, the Manufacturers' Association conceded it, though the Provisional Government and even the Petrograd Soviet protested that this would weaken the war effort. Actually the concession was merely the recognition of an accomplished fact. Workmen had begun to march out of the factories in a body at the end of eight hours' labour.

On 7 March, Paléologue dropped in at an aristocratic tea party on the Serguievskaia.

'The stories told and impressions exchanged revealed the darkest pessimism, but there was one anxiety greater than all the others, a haunting fear in every mind – the partition of the land. "We shall not get out of it *this* time. What will become of us without our rent-rolls?" The company's forebodings comprised not only formal expropriation, but wholesale looting and *jacquerie*. A fresh caller, a lieutenant in the Chevaliers-Gardes, entered the room, wearing the red favour on his tunic. He soothed the company's anxieties a little by arguing that the agrarian question was not as terrifying as it might seem at first sight. "There's no need to have immediate recourse to our estates to take the edge off the peasants' hunger," he said. "With the Crown lands and the Church and monastic lands there's enough to keep the mujiks from gnawing-pains for quite a long time to come." His entire audience agreed with this argument; everyone consoled himself with the thought that the Russian nobility would not suffer too severely if the Emperor, Empress, grand dukes, grand duchesses, the Church and the monasteries were ruthlessly robbed and plundered. As Rochefoucauld said: "We can always find strength to bear the misfortunes of others." '9

Institutional relics of the old order quickly gave their blessing to the new one. They had, of course, very little choice. Thus the Council of Representatives of Trade and Industry, an organization controlled by millionaires, promised unreserved support for the Provisional Committee of the Duma before that body had even declared itself to be the government. On 10 March, the Council of Nobles, traditionally the chief bastion of the Throne, invited the nation to 'close ranks behind the Provisional Government, now the sole legal authority in Russia'.

The Council of Empire, the upper chamber of the Tsarist legislature, did not go into commission like the lower house. Its members, half of them straight nominees of Nicholas II, continued to sit and draw their salaries in the strange new circumstances, and a two-day debate in the Excom resulted in no move to abolish them. Nor, under the Provisional Government, did the Senate abandon its shadowy constitutional role, but sat to approve, in all the solemnity of court dress, a whole series of would-be revolutionary decrees.

Kerensky, as Minister of Justice, did carry out one of the Excom's requests, appointing workers' and soldiers' representatives as assessors in the courts of justice; but few of the Tsarist judges and prosecutors were dismissed.

The Orthodox Church continued to function, though there was no Tsar to defend it. The Provisional Government duly appointed a new Procurator of the Holy Synod, thus exercising the temporal authority over it that Peter the Great had assumed. As individuals, however, many leading churchmen paid dearly for their previous dependence on Rasputin. On 16 March, Paléologue wrote in his memoirs: 'All the metropolitans, archbishops, archimandrites, abbots, archpriests and hieromonachs of whom he had formed his ecclesiastical court are having a bad time. Their own flocks, and often even their subordinates, are rising up against them. Most have resigned their offices, more or less spontaneously; many are in flight, or in prison. The Metropolitan of Petrograd, Pitirim, has obtained leave to expiate his offences in a Siberian monastery.'[10]

Yet the religious habits and feelings of the masses could not be expected to vanish overnight. The funeral ceremonies in the Champ de Mars for the revolutionary victims of the fighting were of a purely civil nature, and for that reason the Cossacks refused to attend them. The following day a growing number of the humbler classes, not excluding many soldiers, began to give expression to these very feelings. They were particularly concerned that the coffins had been painted in the revolutionary red, instead of in the traditional white or yellow. In the end the Provisional Government ordered a number of priests to go to the place and say Christian prayers over the graves.

Amid all this ferment of ideas and aims there was one decisive element that inevitably occupied the forefront of everybody's mind. Russia, in February 1917, had six million men under arms. Units of this vast force had revolted and overturned the State. Yet this same force was engaged in a life-and-death struggle with the Central Powers. War and revolution had kept the same tryst with destiny, tearing apart the Russian soul.

The outbreak of hostilities in 1914 had been welcomed by the Autocracy as providing a focus for reactionary patriotism, by the liberals as a means of modifying the Autocracy by associating it with the parliamentary democracies of Britain and France, and by the revolutionaries as opening up the possibility of still more fundamental change. Now, after two-and-a-half years of fighting, during which the Russian capacity to wage a modern war had been abundantly disproved and two-and-a-half million ill-armed and ill-directed soldiers had perished, these various attitudes to the war had changed.

The Tsar, and indeed the Tsaritsa, had retained their single-minded patriotism, in spite of all the rumours to the contrary. A mystic Slavophilism was essential to their sense of mission; without it they would not have been able to maintain, for themselves, the credibility of their anachronistic role. Some of their immediate entourage may not have shared this attitude; they may have felt that their life of easy privilege could be best secured through the survival of the Russian, Prussian and Austrian empires in a natural alliance against the democracies of Britain, France and the United States, and so worked secretly for a separate peace. This only revealed their misunderstanding of the forces of history. The emperors' club was never a twentieth-century reality, and Nicholas II was clearly right in thinking that he was either a Russian Tsar or nothing.

The Russian liberals soon realized this about themselves. After the February Revolution their support for the war was intensified. Much to their surprise, they were out on a limb. They were fully aware that a victory for the Kaiser would put an end to their democratic pretensions, and that their only chance of entering into their heritage was in the baggage train of the Allies. A victorious Kaiser would have colonized Russia in the name of the Tsar. Thus their fear of defeat turned them, from the very beginning, into hostages of the Soviet.

The socialists were divided, according to their understanding of the tactics and nature of revolution. The 'defensists' believed that the Russian revolution could be completed only if it were prevented from being over-run by German imperialism. The 'defeatists' either hoped to strike a shrewd bargain with the German capitalist devil, or believed that Germany herself was about to take the lead in a world revolution that would make the capitalist war irrelevant.

In practice, everything depended on the Russian army in the field – that army which, from being a hierarchical institution reflecting, and indeed magnifying, the fixed ranks

of society laid down by Peter the Great, had suddenly, with
the Petrograd mutinies, the abdication of its imperial
Commander-in-Chief, the abolition of the death penalty for
desertion and, above all, the promulgation of Order Number
One, reversed its traditional role and became an element of
instability.

Order Number One reached Headquarters at Mogilev on
the same day as the news of Nicholas's abdication. It
revealed to the High Command the terrible truth that they
had been deceived by the liberal politicians in Petrograd.
By urging the Emperor to vacate the Throne, they had not
paved the way to a respectable constitutional monarchy
with the Grand Duke Michael as regent or sovereign, but
had effectively destroyed their own authority either to
support the State they knew or to wage war against its
external enemy.

Order Number One, issued by the Executive Committee
of the Petrograd Soviet and telegraphed to the armies on
all the fronts, called upon every military and naval unit to
elect its own soviet and send representatives to the parent
body in the capital, whose decisions should override those
of the Military Committee of the Duma. It further ruled
that arms were to be guarded by the regimental soviets and
not by the officers, that soldiers, when off duty, should no
longer be required to salute officers and that the familiar form
of address used by officers to rankers should be abandoned.

The Provisional Government, then in process of formation,
was taken unawares by this astute move. When it tried to
withdraw the Order it was too late. Thus at the very outset
of the Revolution the pattern of its future development was
laid down.

The socialist forces were still without Bolshevik leadership. Nevertheless, during all those years when they had
existed underground, while the liberals were preoccupied
either with wordy battles in the Duma, or with the actual
conduct of the war effort through the Voluntary Organizations, they had had time to consider the inner reality of
the coming struggle and to acquire the kind of revolutionary
instinct that taught them how to seize the good moment when
it came.

The purpose of Order Number One was to underwrite the mutiny of the small Petrograd garrison by joining with it in spirit the largest national force engaged in the European war. No courts martial were thereafter to be feared as a sequel to the butchery of officers that had occurred in Petrograd, Kronstadt and Helsingfors. The dumbest peasant soldier realized that everything had changed. The officers could not, in the middle of a war, be immediately replaced, but whether they were reactionary and of noble birth, or liberal-minded wartime recruits from the professional classes, they henceforth disposed of no authority other than that which their training and personality had given them.

The Order, in fact, set in train the rapid dissolution of the Imperial Army. As an institution it played little further part in the war against the Central Powers, nor, ironically enough, in the shaping of the Revolution which a small minority of its personnel had started. As a military force it neither sustained that Revolution nor attempted to reverse it. It turned slowly into a mob of armed and freebooting deserters, until such time as Trotsky remobilized it to fight a civil war.

At the Stavka some semblance of discipline was maintained until after the Bolshevik seizure of power in October. The dethroned Tsar, who was visited from the Crimea by his mother, the Empress Dowager, lingered for a few days before returning in captivity to Tsarskoye Selo. General Alexeiev, the Chief of Staff, arranged a ceremonial farewell for him, at which he quietly thanked the staff officers for their loyalty and begged them to forget any differences between them and lead the army to victory. All in the room cheered, and some wept.

But next morning the same officers assembled to take the oath of allegiance to the Provisional Government. That night, the little garrison town was illuminated, and crowds stayed up to celebrate in the streets. The officers began to remove the imperial monogram from their epaulettes, and aides-de-camp to cut away their golden shoulder-knots.

In Petrograd itself, when most of the mutineers had ceased careering about the city and returned to barracks, General Kornilov, the new Military Governor, did make an attempt to show that military discipline had been restored. On Sunday, 19 March, he ordered a review of troops on the Winter Palace Square, selecting for this only the least unruly elements. It was the first time since the Revolution that a substantial force had been assembled in regular formation, and Allied ambassadors were invited to watch from the Foreign Ministry. Paléologue described the scene: 'The troops – ten thousand men or so – had a tolerable soldierly bearing and marched past in good order. There were very few officers. All the bands played the *Marseillaise*, but at a slow pace, which made it sound sinister. In each company and squadron I noticed several red banners bearing inscriptions: "Land and Liberty", "The Land for the People", "Long Live the Socialist Republic". On a very small number I read: "The War until Victory." '[11]

Lieutenant Prince Lobanov-Rostovsky, of the Sapper Guards, was recovering from malaria in a hospital behind the lines at Volhynia when the Revolution broke out. On 1 March, he was ordered to complete his convalescence with his regiment's reserve battalion in Petrograd. At that time confused rumours from the capital had reached his sector. Lobanov observed that the officers in his unit had begun 'to reveal themselves under their uniforms',[12] displaying amazingly different political views and feelings; the men had seemed quite unconcerned about events. It must have been a surprise to him, therefore, when he awaited the Petrograd connection in the first-class railway restaurant at Kiev, to watch a mob break in to remove the portrait of the Tsar and all other imperial insignia.

He received another shock on the Petrograd express. Some of the military guards on board, wearing red ribbons on their caps, invaded the first-class carriages, smoking and shouting. 'A new picture for Russia,'[13] the Prince recorded.

Petrograd was reached in the small hours of 5 March. There were no cabs to be seen, and Lobanov decided to walk through the deserted streets to the smart Astoria Hotel which, early in the war, had been commandeered for the accommodation of important military missions. He expected to find his uncle, who was Assistant Chief of the Naval

Staff. The building was in complete darkness, and its plate-glass windows were smashed. When he knocked at a side door it was opened by armed sailors, who immediately arrested him for carrying a revolver and not having a pass. Eventually a nervous young naval lieutenant arrived, and, after some hesitation, said to the sailors nominally under his command: 'Comrades, let this man out. He has just arrived, and didn't know there was a revolution.' Reluctantly they agreed to release him.

Lobanov found his uncle and aunt at the Admiralty, where they had taken refuge during the attack on the hotel. Next day he went to report to the commander of the reserve battalion in its barracks.

'The familiar buildings and parade ground looked empty. At the gate I saw a soldier sitting with a rifle across his knees and puffing at a cigarette. He wore no belt. For over a century there had not been an instant, day or night, that a sentry had not stood at that point, trim, rigid, erect, the very embodiment of discipline. As you passed he would salute you with mechanical precision. In this slovenly, bedraggled fellow who was now sitting in his place I could not help seeing a symbol of the disappearance of an important historical era.'[14]

It turned out that the battalion commander, Colonel Ivanov, had been wounded by his own troops two days before, that another officer, Captain Romanov, had been arrested because of his name (though he was no relation of the imperial house), and that five of the other officers of the battalion had gone into hiding. A single lieutenant had been left in charge, but another officer of the regiment, Captain Bronevsky, had happened to arrive on leave from the front, and had been elected by the soldiers' committee to take command. Captain Bronevsky told Prince Lobanov: 'You are a prisoner here until your fate is decided, and that will depend on your popularity. They will do one of three things: attempt to murder you, put you in prison or elect you one of their officers.'[15]

Lobanov was elected, and made adjutant of the battalion. He found that to administer a thousand unruly men, under the conditions of Order Number One, was a tougher assignment than any he had experienced in the face of the enemy. On 15 March, for example, he noted in his diary:

'Some drunken members of the committee entered the officers' mess and smashed the billiard tables. While passing through the main entrance of the barracks I saw that the sentry had quietly put down his rifle and gone away. As I was walking down the street I saw the Kexholm Guards Regiment passing by; I stopped to salute the colours and was immediately surrounded by a crowd of soldiers who began booing me violently and calling me a counter-revolutionary. I further noted that the streets were crowded with idly sauntering soldiers. They seemed to take special pleasure in riding on the trams, and every one that passed had bunches of uniformed men hanging on to it.'[16]

On 25 March, the Volhynian Regiment, formerly a regiment of the Guard, which had been the first to revolt on 27 February, organized a concert at the Mariinsky Theatre for the benefit of revolutionary victims of the fighting. The Allied ambassadors were invited on this occasion, and thought it wise to attend. The Provisional Government was there in full force. Here Paléologue noted another contrast: 'What an extraordinary change at the Mariinsky Theatre!' he wrote. 'Could its clever stage-hands have succeeded in producing such an amazing transformation?'[17]

All the imperial coats of arms and golden eagles had been removed. The box attendants had exchanged their sumptuous Court liveries for dirty grey jackets. Part of the audience was still bourgeois, but students and soldiers had also acquired tickets.

The ambassadors occupied the box of the imperial family; opposite them, in the Minister of the Court's box, were the new ministers in frock coats. The great imperial box itself, in the centre, was occupied by some thirty persons, old men and women, victims of Tsarist terrorism, who scarcely three weeks before had been living in exile in Siberia or in the fortress prison of St Peter and St Paul.

When Vera Figner, the old Nihilist leader, appeared on the conductor's rostrum, dressed in a black woollen gown and a white fichu, to remind the company, without any sign of rancour, of the countless army of obscure victims who had bought the present triumph of the Revolution with their lives, even Paléologue was moved.

'The concluding phrases struck an indescribable note of sadness, resignation and pity. Perhaps the Slav soul alone is capable of that intensity. A funeral march which the orchestra at once began seemed a continuation of the speech, the effect of which thus culminated in religious emotion. Most of those present were reduced to tears.

'It was time to go. The ceremony had made a peculiarly poignant impression on us; we did not want to spoil it. In the empty passages through which I hastened I seemed to see the ghosts of my smart women friends who had so often been here to lull their restless minds with the novelties of the ballet, and who were the last attraction of a social system that has vanished for ever.'[18]

In those early days Vladimir Korostovetz had an opportunity of observing the attempted emergence of a somewhat different social system. As a senior member of the Foreign Ministry he had been appointed to act as liaison between the old bureaucratic machine and Milyukov, his new minister. Part of his duty was to vet the people who came to the ministry to offer their services to the new regime.

'The waiting-rooms were full from morning to night. All made a great to-do about what they had done for the Revolution and of their persecution by the Tsarist Government. All were armed with "recommendations" and letters from sections and sub-sections of the organizations that had sprung up like mushrooms after rain all around the Soviets. And who indeed was not to be found among the petitioners? Political emigrés only just returned home; international spies; lunatics; actresses who wished to become revolutionary heroines; even Badmayev, the friend of Rasputin; then members of all kinds of Czech and Polish organizations; Bulgars who asserted they had fled from their country because their criminal Government had lifted its hand against "Bulgaria's liberator"; Tibetan and Mongolian explorers; countless foreign professors and socialists who had come to the Promised Land of Revolution.'[19]

Paléologue was surprised at the number of prominent members of the old regime who began to haunt the ante-chambers of the Provisional Government, offering their help and suggesting with calm effrontery that the prestige of their name or the worth of their talents would be of inestimable advantage to the new regime. He conceded that some of these people contemplated changing sides from motives of patriotism, believing that the only way to prevent anarchy was to rally round what was left of sound govern-ance in Russia.

Sukhanov saw this differently. He believed that the Russian bourgeoisie, unlike those involved in attempted revolutions in other countries, had betrayed the people not the day after the overturn, but before the overturn took place. 'They had not started the Revolution with the intention of turning against the people at an opportune moment, but had been dragged by the hair into the movement when the people's revolution had already developed to its full extent. This bourgeoisie of ours left no room for doubt as to their goals. We had to keep our ears and eyes open if we did not want to exchange one Duma Protopopov under Tsar Nicholas for another.'[20]

In fact, there was no bourgeois strategy in those early days, and no unity of thought. Many families were divided. Elisaveta Fen, who was a university student then, recorded that while her father, a retired high civil servant at Mogilev, distrusted the new government from the start, her sister, in common with the majority of university-educated people, believed that the overthrow of the monarchy had opened the way to political and social changes that were long overdue. 'The exchange of views between them frequently took the form of violent quarrels. Until then I had known only the gentle, almost timid side of my sister's character, and it shocked and alarmed me to see her turning against my father, to hear her say such hard things to him, taunting him with having been a servant of "the rotten monarchy". He re-torted with no less violence that it was *her* revolutionaries who were rotten, nay, criminal. As they raised their voices at one another my mother would step in, attempting to conciliate, and would point out to my sister that she should

not speak to her father as she did. My sister would then
charge my mother with being unfair to her, and would leave
the room, trembling with indignation and wounded pride.'[21]

The first fine careless rapture did not last long. It gave
way to fear among the haves and frustration among the
have-nots. Moreover, so far as the former were concerned,
hints in many memoirs bear out the subtle judgement that
Pasternak attributed to Dr Zhivago, who, returning to
Moscow from the front after the February Revolution, found
his pre-war bourgeois friends 'strangely dim and colour-
less'. He felt he must have over-estimated them in the past.
'It had been easy enough to do so, as long as the order of
things had been such that people with means could indulge
their follies and eccentricities at the expense of the poor.
The fooling, the right to idleness enjoyed by the few while
the majority suffered, could itself create an illusion of
genuine character and orginality. But how quickly, once
the lower classes had risen and the rich had lost their
privileges, had these people faded!'[22]

Their distractions became as frenzied as those of the
aristocrats who had disported themselves in Rasputin's
company. Paustovsky wrote that in Moscow the bourgeoisie
frequented gypsy night-clubs, sectarian chapels and gambling dens, and patronized 'howling mobs of aesthetes' who
met at Persov's near St Saviour's Church.

At a lower level, among those educated persons who had
liked to think of themselves as radicals, the new aim was to
jump on to the Soviet bandwagon by joining the Social
Revolutionary Party. These were the 'March socialists' who
aroused the contempt of the future rulers of Russia. Their
adherence to what had been a mass party of peasants and
workers led by a cadre of genuine revolutionaries gave it a
distinctly petty-bourgeois appearance, and soon led to a
split. Eventually the Left S.R.s were absorbed into the
Bolshevik ranks; the Right S.R.s were annihilated.

At this time, however, they were needed. M. P. Price,
correspondent for the *Manchester Guardian*, observed how
many officers, advocates, middle-class politicians, journalists
and small government officials were elected to the Moscow
Soviet, simply because that body had as yet no confidence in

itself and welcomed recruits with some experience of public life. Anyone from the liberal professions, and anyone with a university degree who was not positively known to be a monarchist, could get into the Social Revolutionary Party.

The sudden shift in the political spectrum had left the Cadets, who had partially instigated the Revolution but had by no means carried it out, on the far Right of effective political life. The old Right, including the organizers of the Black Hundreds, had gone underground, and the Octobrists, who had represented the more liberal elements of the land-owning class, had, as a party, no further function. It was the Cadets, once considered so radical, who were called upon to occupy the conservative position. They were the party that still possessed funds, the party of the bankers and the millionaire industrialists. They were the only people, at first, capable of taking control of what remained of the old State machine, and so they formed the Provisional Government which was to hold the ring until a freely elected Constitutional Assembly could decide the future of the Empire. They were no longer constitutional monarchists, for they feared that any kind of restoration might bring back the *status quo ante*. In theory they had espoused the Revolution, but they earnestly hoped to keep it within bounds; and they used the war as an excuse for postponing a final settlement of the agrarian question and the establishment of social justice.

The prospect was far from encouraging. Endless problems assailed them, to solve which they needed the support of the Soviet. Nor were there any sure guidelines, when all society was in a state of flux.

But the sorting-out process was about to begin. On 3 April, Easter Monday, Lenin arrived at the Finland Station.

6

Dyarchy

'Easter!' exclaimed Count Lucien de Robien, of the French Embassy, describing the weekend before Lenin arrived. 'All the windows of the Preobrajensky barracks were lit up. All the church bells were ringing, and the cannon of the Fortress were firing salvoes. The events of the last weeks seemed like a bad dream. It was the Russia of old, risen again with Christ.'[1]

Robien went to a supper party at Princess Gorchakov's, where the elegance and splendour heightened his impression. 'The women, who had just come from the Easter services, were in pure white evening dresses. Some of them wore long necklaces of miniature enamelled Easter eggs. The table was laden with food, not forgetting the *pashka* and the little pig with the woe-begone expression. Gorchakov had fetched the best bottles from his cellar.'[2]

The first post-revolutionary Holy Week had followed the customary pattern, except that the theatres, which formerly were closed in the last two weeks of Lent, stayed open until the eve of Maundy Thursday. The Easter Liturgy itself was celebrated with the usual splendour, but, in the absence of the Metropolitan Pitrim, imprisoned in his Siberian monastery, the pontifical Mass at the monastery of St Alexander Nevsky was sung by Metropolitan Tikhon. The crowds in the great Petrograd cathedrals were as great as in former

93

years, but in the working class quarters of the city the
churches were practically empty.

There were a few more parties to come, for those who
had formerly lived it up so carelessly. On 12 April Robien
went to a 'very *ancien régime* concert' in the Fontanka Palace.
'The eagles were still there, and there was a portrait of
Peter the Great at the end of the room. All the familiar
faces in the audience. The officers had almost all put back
their epaulettes, as there was no danger in showing them in
this place and one could hide them under an overcoat when
going outside. The women were in low cut dresses. One
could have believed it was before the Revolution. This
entr'acte amused me.'[3]

Two days later Robien's chief, Paléologue, joined a family
dinner party in the Grand Duke Paul's palace at Tsarskoye
Selo. The host was in a general's uniform, but he had
removed his aide-de-camp's shoulder-knot and the imperial
monogram on his St George's Cross.

'He has preserved his calm and unaffected dignity, but
lines of woe are deeply etched upon his haggard face.
Princess Paley was deeply trembling with grief and exasperation. As we walked through the rooms on the way to dinner
the same thought struck us all simultaneously. We feasted
our eyes on all this splendour, the pictures, the tapestries,
the profusion of furniture and art treasures. What was the
good of all that now? What would become of all these
marvels and glories? With tears in her eyes, the poor
Princess said to me: "Perhaps this house will be taken from
us quite soon – and I've put so much of myself into it." '[4]

Countess Kleinmichel, still out of favour with the leaders
of the Provisional Government, suffered again. In the
middle of March a group of thirty-three soldiers arrived at
her mansion with a warrant from the Petrograd Soviet to
hold her under house arrest. They were joined later by
fifteen sailors. The soldiers made a rifle-range on the stairs,
using portraits of the Romanovs as targets. They put
cigarettes in the mouth of the Tsaritsa Elisabeth and cut the
nose of Catherine II. They let no one into the house, not
even the Countess's doctor. They stole part of her silver. Her
big drawing-room was turned into a meeting-place for the

area section of the Workers' and Soldiers' Committee, where her dainty pink chairs were set round a trestle table. Visited by Robien after forty days of this treatment, she told him that she felt she would kill herself if fresh troubles arose, rather than submit to the fate of her nephew, an officer at Louga, who, after seeing two of his friends murdered, was killed by being blinded and having his hands cut off.

The Countess observed that her servants, irritated by their long imprisonment and corrupted by the speeches of agitators who succeeded one another in her ballroom, were obviously much changed.

'They had all been in my service for long years; I had seen some of them married, and we had formed a family whose bond had seemed unbreakable. But they were soon embittered by a captivity for which they held me to account, and exacted enormous compensation in money. It was both comical and sad to see them waiting on me at luncheon and dinner in liveries adorned with red bows, repeating to me the first principles of the Revolution.'[5]

As for these 'first principles of the Revolution', they were at that time very much in dispute. Each man had his own set, and there were orators at every street corner to shout out their own. But Lenin had arrived, completing in his 'sealed train' what was surely the most fateful railway journey in history. The bourgeoisie watched helplessly as he took charge of the situation, beginning to undermine the frail compromise by which such authority as existed was divided at the centre between the Provisional Government and the Soviet.

The young Princess Zinaida Shakhovskoi, whose education at the Catherine Institute had been interrupted by events, was living in a Petrograd flat with her family. She remembers that one day her mother, crossing one of the squares, was attracted by the sight of a political meeting.

'She moved closer, so that she could hear the speaker: it was Lenin. The look of the man and the things he said made such an impression on her that she paid a call on Prince Lvov, whom she knew well.

' "It's nothing," said Lvov. "Don't worry; we've got our eyes on him. He's harmless enough."

'My mother told him of her plan to take her children to Sweden.

' "No," replied the Prince gravely, "you mustn't do that. It's your duty to stay here; go down to your estates and help the Russian people to acclimatize themselves to their new condition."

'Since it was her duty, my mother buried herself—and us— in the heart of Russia.'[6]

During this period a pathetic band of once-powerful Tsarist personages – ministers, Court officers, generals, bishops, police chiefs and associates of Rasputin – were brought out blinking, one by one, from the Peter-Paul Fortress to give evidence to the Muravyev enquiry into the conduct, at the top, of the fallen regime. They were not on trial, and they were questioned gently, but their distress was apparent to all. Most of them tried to pretend that they had had very little influence on affairs, and Protopopov's account of his stewardship as the Tsar's last Minister of the Interior almost gave the impression that this crucial office had been a sinecure. Nevertheless, a number of Byzantine scandals in high places were revealed which would have fascinated the public if they had not had other things to think about.

The Commission's report was never published. It had not completed its work when the Bolsheviks seized power, and they dissolved it as irrelevant. This did not save most of the witnesses from being executed, sooner or later.

In April an all-Russian conference of soviets assembled in Petrograd, thereby signifying that the Revolution was a truly national event. Lenin treated it to his famous 'April Theses'. He demanded that the Provisional Government be replaced by a Republic of the Proletariat and that capitalism, still the economic basis of Russian society, be completely overthrown. Land must be nationalized, the State must control all production and there must be one nationalized bank. Soldiers at the front should fraternize with the Germans, in furtherance of total revolution, first in the Kaiser's Germany and then in the whole world.

This was the first formal, serious and immediate challenge to the economic *status quo*, and it was naturally resisted by those as yet unready for such a breathtaking leap into the future. Though there was a larger Bolshevik representation at the Conference than anyone might have expected six weeks before, Lenin's programme was rejected. Nevertheless, its formulation, with its powerful appeal to the masses, put everything into disarray, and made an orderly consummation of the Revolution, whether on liberal or moderate socialist lines, impossible.

The result was increasing anarchy, against which the bourgeoisie, to whom this was especially horrifying, struggled in vain. Putilov, the big industrialist, realizing that the economy of the country was on the verge of collapse, founded a Society for the Economic Rehabilitation of Russia. It had the political aim of supporting moderate bourgeois candidates for the forthcoming Constituent Assembly. Its well-heeled members had money and influence at the top, but in the end they were unable to resist the forces Lenin had released from below. As Trotsky remarked, the possession of wealth is effective only when society underwrites it.

The Provisional Government possessed no means of countering the insidious propaganda of the Bolsheviks. Dimly realizing that it had played the role of the Sorcerer's Apprentice, it tried to reverse the flood – with lecture tours. The Union of Zemstvos invited eminent dons and literary men to go round the country giving explanatory talks on the political reorganization of Russia. It was an attempt to educate rather than indoctrinate, but it was like teaching lifeboat drill while the ship was sinking. A Government survey in May remarked sorrowfully that in the rural areas 'the more conscientious the writers are in their endeavours to present the subject lucidly, the more capable and cultured they are, the worse is the result. A stone is offered where bread is asked for.'

The Provisional Government's 'commissars' soon became unpopular. They were the kind of people who had helped the peasants in the past, but they were seen in a different light when they were supposed to represent authority. Before they had been, at least by implication, opposed to the powers-that-be; now, in a fluid situation, they spoke in their name, which was another thing altogether.

The middle classes themselves were scarcely more receptive. A 'League of Personal Example' was founded to encourage the educated community in general to accept a more positive role in the regeneration of society. Sir Bernard Pares, who took part in this for a time, wrote: 'We felt our meetings did not make much difference to things. We could always get a hall for nothing; it was always crammed; people always clapped vehemently; as a rule the other side did not show up; and at the end they all went off and no doubt simply asked themselves how soon we should have peace. The bourgeois were particuarly annoying in this respect; they seemed to have no initiative.'[7]

Pares would have felt happier if such people had had sharper convictions of any kind, and stood up for them more vehemently.

The anarchy was present in the cities, where the new Red Guards, replacing the Tsarist police, were unable or unwilling to prevent the illegal occupation of abandoned mansions by various revolutionary groups, including anarchists. It was present in the countryside, where the Provisional Government's 'land commissioners' often found it impossible to restrain the peasantry from anticipating the land redistribution which, in theory, was to be left to the future Constituent Assembly to initiate. It was present in the central bureaucracy which, though still composed largely of the old Tsarist personnel, was faced with the task of carrying out administrative policies which the new ministers, like corks bobbing about in a whirlpool, changed every other day. Above all, it was present at the front, where the abolition of the death penalty was leading to wholesale desertions by peasant-soldiers anxious to return home and claim their share of the Revolution's bounty.

Indiscipline spread in odd ways as the bonds that had held society together weakened. At Petrograd University a group of students elected a committee which demanded soup for breakfast, with hot chocolate on Sundays and Thursdays, and the right to get up an hour later and to stay up until ten at night. When their demands were refused, they marched off to the Duma, where a minister congratulated them on their spirit of organization.

Countess Adam Lamoyska, arriving in Petrograd from
Kiev, reported that she dared not return to her family place
at Petchara, in Podolia. Hitherto, she told her friends, the
peasants had all been faithful and attached to her mother.
But since the Revolution everything had changed. They
stood at the mansion gate or in the park, pretending to
divide up the seigneurial lands in dumb show. One of them
would affect to want the woods by the river; another would
put in for the gardens to turn into sheepfolds. 'They talked
like this for hours, not even stopping when the gentry
approached them.'

Young Prince Lobanov-Rostovsky, by now a captain,
was at this time still struggling with his unenviable job as
adjutant of an unruly regiment in Petrograd. The temper
of the men was shown when he secured a lucrative contract
for the regimental band, which was otherwise idle, to play
in the evenings at Zon, a summer garden where a vaudeville
show was given in the open air. When the soldiers' committee
learned that the bourgeoisie as well as proletarians attended
the performances, they sternly instructed the bandsmen to
forego this addition to their pay.

The young prince, who came from a famous diplomatic
family, used the magnificent library of his vastly rich god-
father, Count Andrei Bobrinsky, a descendant of Catherine
the Great, to make a study of revolutions. The stories of
Marius and Sulla in Rome, of Cromwell's Commonwealth,
of the great French Revolution and of the Revolutions of
1848 were all grist to his mill.

'I passed many hours jotting down what I called the general
principles governing revolutions and trying to make out a
chart that would apply to the course of events in Russia.
With the self-assurance of youth I believed too implicitly
in the immutability of the laws of history and thought
one could gauge coming events with mathematical precision.

'By the beginning of May I came to the following conclusion: This revolution was only beginning, and, what was
worse, it was changing from a purely political one to a social
one. Much bloodshed, and possibly terror, were ahead of

us. I belonged to the privileged class which was bound to be destroyed. The time would come when, together with all other members of this class, I should be accused of dreadful crimes against the nation. How I could have committed these crimes personally would have been difficult to say, since I had gone to war directly from the schoolroom, but in the terror phase revolutions are dominated by hatreds and not by reason. Passing by the city slaughterhouse one day, and seeing the blissfully ignorant expressions of the sheep being driven into it, I could not help comparing myself and all my friends with these doomed animals.

'What could be done about it? Revolutions could be divided into two periods – the destructive period, followed by the constructive period. Therefore the thing to do was to get out of the country at the beginning of the terror and come back when the hatreds had subsided into the enthusiasm of reconstruction.

'To make a comparison with the French Revolution, which I took as the archetype, it meant emigrating just before the death of Louis XVI and coming back after the 9th Thermidor at the beginning of the Directory period. The whole problem at the moment consisted in gauging the time rightly. Estimating that I had some four or five months ahead of me, I decided to begin looking around for opportunities to get out of what I called the lunatic asylum – Petrograd. As we were still at war, there was one obvious course of action – to have myself appointed to some foreign front. There I could weather the storm or perhaps, if circumstances forced or permitted, join one of the Allied armies. The vision of a normal disciplined front appeared to me as paradise compared with the hotbed of anarchy in which I found myself.

'Once my mind was made up on this point I began looking for a vacancy. During my free hours I visited the General Staff. That supreme sanctuary of the army had formerly been strictly closed to all but the chosen few, who were admitted by pass only. Now it was a kind of bazaar. The vast halls of the great building were crowded with a loafing mass of soldiers, among whom I supposed there must be a number of spies. How any strategical operations could be planned, or secrets kept, in this din and noise was a mystery to me.'[8]

Eventually Lobanov found a chance vacancy in a newly formed battalion destined for Salonika. It had its full complement of officers, but few privates.

'When I told my comrades there was an outcry of horror. It was sheer madness. I was leaving a Guards regiment to go among God knew what riffraff. The battalion would never leave Russia, and, even if it did, I should probably be murdered on the way.'[9]

The regimental soldiers' committee objected to Lobanov's secondment, and he had to slip out of the barracks when they were empty. He spent a month recruiting volunteers.

'On the whole I was pleased with the type of men we were getting. They were mostly university students or old N.C.O.s who would avow in a whisper that they were joining us to get away from the increasing anarchy and confusion of Petrograd. Occasionally curious types presented themselves. One man said he had been wounded at the front, and, when I asked him whether he had any papers to prove it, silently took out his glass eye and laid it on the table. Another stated that he had been an interpreter on the Swedish border and declared he could speak several languages. He looked like a rugged illiterate *mujik*, so I became suspicious and asked if he knew Italian. He took a small edition of Petrarch out of his pocket and handed it to me. I was so impressed that I enrolled him. This was a mistake, as I discovered when he became one of the leaders of the revolutionary committee which roused the men against us.'[10]

Lobanov's salary ceased when he left the Guards, as the embryo battalion did not yet have a paymaster. His family, who were abroad, could no longer transfer funds, and his own resources in Russia consisted of now-worthless bonds.

'The result was that I starved amidst plenty. I was living in the magnificent house of the Bobrinskys, but the whole family was away and I was alone. Around me was a whole staff of over-fed servants, but I did not want to ask them to prepare meals for me. When dinnertime came I would go out punctually as if to a neighbouring restaurant; but, having counted my money, I decided to have dinner only every other day.'[11]

On the off-days Lobanov would sit through the dinner hour in one of the public parks, reflecting on the deep pall of gloom and fear that was creeping over Petrograd. He recalled a poster put up by the Provisional Government in March: 'There is a known path for revolutions that leads through bloodshed and terror to dictatorship.'

In October, Lobanov did reach the Salonika front, but his many subsequent adventures belied his painstaking interpretation of the natural course of revolutions. If not Marx, then Lenin or Trotsky, would have corrected his theorizing. There was no 9th Thermidor in Russia, and when the prince eventually returned to Russian soil in January 1919 and joined the White forces in the Crimea, he was back, according to his historical analogies, in the hapless frustration of the French royalists at Coblenz. On the day when, according to his earlier calculations, he had planned to return to a resurrected Russia, he shared in the Allied evacuation of Novorossiisk, and never saw her shores again.

Meanwhile, in April 1917, the Revolution had arrived at an uncomfortable pause, satisfactory to nobody. It was as though the two sides were flexing their muscles, preparing for the full encounter. There was, however, a kind of no-man's-land between them, where individual blossoms, like Flanders poppies, made a fitful appearance. All classes took part, as they had been unable to do under Tsarism, expressing their ideas through clubs and corporations, political, professional, religious and ethnic associations. They turned instinctively to the Soviet. The release of pent-up social ambitions resulted in processions of dissident Christians, Jews, Muslims, Buddhists, school teachers, apprentices, orphans, midwives, and even prostitutes.

The first May Day of the Revolution (observed on 18 April, Old Style, to concide with such celebrations in the West) was a curiously mixed affair. At Mogilev it was the Knights of St George who led the military procession, accompanied by all the remaining Tsarist generals, but in Petrograd and Moscow the workers dominated the occasion. Across the façade of the Mariinsky Palace, now the seat of the Provisional Government, hung a giant red banner carrying the words: 'Long Live the Third International!' Trotsky, uncharacteristically, was moved by the universality of the celebration. 'The different strata of the population contributed their own quality to the holiday, but all flowed into a whole, very loosely held together and partly false, but on the whole majestic.'[12]

Artists, at this stage, had not yet got their bearings, but the old dignified art world had collapsed. There was an exhibition of Finnish painting at the beginning of April, attended by the entire élite of Petrograd – ministers, Duma deputies, painters, artists, writers. When Milyukov, as Foreign Minister, rose to propose the official toast, Mayakovsky, the anarchic poet, jumped on a chair and shouted him down. The French Ambassador rebuked him, but he shouted even louder, while pandemonium broke out among his companions. Gorky, who was present, was said to be greatly amused.

Standards of public decorum changed rapidly. When Kerensky lunched at the French Embassy he wore a coat unbuttoned to the neck, without collar or tie. A member of the staff described him as 'neither bourgeois, nor workman or soldier'. On arrival he shook hands with the footman.

Shortly afterwards, the articulate French Ambassador, Paléologue, was appointed to a new post. Before leaving he paid a farewell visit to the Grand Duke Nicholas Michaelovitch.

'Not much was left of the splendid optimism he affected at the dawn of the new order. He made no attempt to conceal his grief and anxiety. His voice trembled as he took me through to the vestibule. "When we meet again," he said, "where will Russia have got to? Shall we ever meet again?"

"You're in a very gloomy mood, Monseigneur."

"How can you expect me to forget that I am marked down for the gallows?"'[13]

By this time most of Paléologue's aristocratic circle of Petrograd friends had vanished. Some had left for Moscow, where the atmosphere for the moment was less menacing; others had gone to their estates, hoping thereby to regain the loyalty of their peasants; others, more fearful, had taken refuge in Sweden. The Ambassador was able to round up only a dozen for his farewell dinner party. 'Everyone seemed absorbed in his own thoughts, and the atmosphere was doleful.'[14]

Well it might be. The bourgeois government, engaging at last in an open trial of strength with the Soviet, had now publicly shown its total incapacity to control events. Foreign Minister Milyukov's Note to the Allies, assuring them of Russia's continued determination to fight the war to its conclusion and to honour all her treaty obligations, was the one thing calculated to unite the socialists against the Cadets. 'Defensists' many of the Right S.R.s and Mensheviks might be, so far as protecting the Revolution from Imperial Germany was concerned, but none of them wanted to fight a 'capitalist' war.

So history repeated itself, this time, in Marx's phrase, as a farce. The Finnish Regiment appeared threateningly before the Mariinsky Palace – another mutiny! Crowds came out again on the streets, shouting abuse at ministers. There was some sporadic shooting, but Prince Lvov's government proved to be even weaker than the Tsar's. Kornilov, the right-wing Military Governor, was forbidden to use force, and he left for the front in disgust. Milyukov was obliged to explain away his offending Note, and to accept in principle the Soviet's policy of 'peace without annexations or indemnities'.

Such was the end of the absurd anomaly by which a group of frock-coated gentlemen, deriving their authority, such as it was, from the Tsarist past, had pretended to rule Russia by and with the consent of the Soviet. A coalition was now inevitable; there was nothing for it but to admit representatives of the socialist parties to the nominal seats of power.

The respectable Prince Lvov stayed formally at the helm, presiding over a cabinet consisting of nine liberals and six moderate socialists. Nothing less would have met the situation, but it was a mutual kiss of death. By uniting and so sharing the responsibility for governing in impossible conditions, the liberals and the majority of the Soviet laid themselves open to direct attack by the Bolsheviks. The liberals had to sacrifice their two best leaders, Milyukov and Guchkov; the Soviet lost its position as the natural standard-bearer of the Revolution. Everything, in other words, was going Lenin's way. As Sir Robert Bruce Lockhart put it: 'The dual power which had existed from the first had strangled all decision, for, while the Soviet refused to govern, it would not allow the Provisional Ministers to do so. In a period when days were equal to months, valuable and irretrievable time was lost in a spate of repetitious speechifying. It was difficult to believe that such a situation could last.'[15]

On 3 May a handful of his modish acquaintances came to see Paléologue off at the station, on his way home to Paris via Stockholm. He was to have been accompanied by his old friend Sazanov, the former Tsarist Foreign Minister, who had been appointed Ambassador in London. But Sazanov arrived to say that his mission has been cancelled. The socialists in the new coalition had no use for former Tsarist ministers.

News came instead of Milyukov's resignation as Foreign Minister. Guchkov had already resigned the War Ministry on the grounds that the conditions under which supreme authority was now being held 'threatened to have consequences fatal to the liberty, safety and indeed to the very existence of Russia'.

Paléologue wrote in his diary: 'This means the final bankruptcy of Russian liberalism and the approaching triumph of the Soviet'.[16] He was right on the first count, but wrong on the second. It was not the divided Soviet that triumphed, but the united Bolshevik Party.

7

Coalition

At first the bourgeoisie took some comfort from the prospect
of life under a coalition. With the end of the Dual Government, the period of double vision ended for Russia and the
struggle for the control of the Revolution could be more
sharply discerned by those who still wielded economic
power. The propertied classes could now at least see where
they stood. From supporting the Provisional Government
in its unresolved and unresolvable conflict with the Soviet they
turned to the more politically congenial task of supporting
the liberal majority in the Provisional Government itself.
The State power, split in two since February, had come into
visible unity again, and so, it would seem, provided an
arena in which the bourgeoisie could further their interests
in the manner to which they were accustomed.

Things did not work out that way. The socialists in the
Cabinet, though in a minority there, had the masses behind
them, until these gradually went over to the Bolsheviks;
and, although the Central Soviet had lost some of its
prestige, Government decrees could not be carried out
without the support of the local soviets, now well established
all over the country. Deprived in government of their
natural leader Milyukov – and of his policy of all-out
loyalty to the Allies – the Cadets were divided over their
immediate political aims. Their liberal dream was rapidly

turning into a nightmare, and the question was whether the better way out was to push the Revolution forward to a point at which it might become stabilized or to restrain it and attempt to return to first base. The Cadets held a party convention in an attempt to orientate themselves. With ex-minister Milyukov as chairman, it only revealed their weakness. Still the party of economic power, they were rapidly losing their grip on political developments.

This was shown in the first fully democratic elections ever to be held in Russia. The Government had decided to reconstitute the municipal dumas on a basis of universal suffrage. In Petrograd itself the Cadets secured only 185 seats out of 801, against the Bolsheviks' 156. The middle ground was held by the S.R.s and Mensheviks, who, however, were divided over support for the Coalition, leaving this vital question in the balance so far as the capital city's government was concerned. This pattern was reproduced in most of the other large towns.

In the country as a whole, however, this stage of political development had not yet been reached. When the First Congress of Soviets assembled on 3 June, it was found to contain a large pro-Coalition majority. The bourgeoisie, of course, were not directly represented in this particular all-Russian gathering, which was the embodiment of the democratic will of twenty million workers and soldiers. Dominated by Social-Revolutionaries (the Bolsheviks and their supporters commanded less than a fifth of the seats), the Congress declined Lenin's exhortation to seize power, gave its general approval to the Coalition, and declared itself in favour of continuing a 'defensive' war.

'At this critical moment,' said Tseretelli, the Menshevik leader, 'not one social force ought to be thrown out of the scales, so long as it may be useful to the cause of the people.'

The Bolsheviks had by this time begun to regard the Mensheviks and Right S.R.s as scarcely distinguishable from the bourgeoisie. These parties now included the 'March socialists' and a great number of that 'third element', educated but at the bottom of the Tsarist pyramid, who in former times had so earnestly attempted to bridge the gap between the haves and the have-nots. These doctors,

veterinary surgeons, school teachers, minor civil servants
and small tradesmen dominated the Congress of Soviets
simply because they could read, write and speak better
than most of the genuine workers. Nicholas Sukhanov, whose
contemporary record of these events is invaluable, estimated
that there were more than a hundred junior officers among
the 820 delegates.

'Judging by their sympathies and by quite intangible
factors',[1] he surmised the presence of a number of secret
Cadets and Octobrists.

Leon Trotsky, referring to the period in June when the
Congress voted for the disarming of the Bolsheviks, wrote:
'These democratic gentlemen, among whom were well-read
people, had invariably given their sympathy to the disarmed,
not to the disarmers – so long as it was a question of reading
old books. But when this question presented itself in reality
they did not recognize it.'[2]

But Trotsky admitted that Tseretelli, from his point of
view, was right.

'To carry the compromise policy through to a successful
end – that is, to the establishment of a parliamentary rule
of the bourgeoisie – demanded the disarmament of the
workers and soldiers. But Tseretelli was not only right; he
was powerless. Neither the soldiers nor the workers would
have voluntarily given up their arms. It would have been
necessary to use force against them. But Tseretelli was
already without force. He could procure it, if at all, only
from the hands of the reaction. But they, in case of a successful crushing of the Bolsheviks, would have immediately
taken up the job of crushing the compromise soviets, and
would not have failed to remind Tseretelli that he was a
former hard-labour convict and nothing more.'[3]

Or, as Sukhanov put it:

'The leaders of the petty-bourgeois S.R. masses proved
faithful to the nature of their party. Flabby creatures without
political personality, caught between the mighty millstones

of capitalist society, they were bewildered by the dizzying events and failed to grasp their meaning. Buffeted by the tempest and shackled by the traditions and fetters of capitalist dictatorship, they cravenly renounced their own minimum programme and surrendered, with the Revolution and the popular masses into the bargain, to the mercy of the bourgeoisie. But in doing this they also lost these popular masses, who rejected their leaders and trampled them into the mud. When the masses saw with their own eyes that their leaders were incompetent and deceitful, and were not leading them forward, the petty-bourgeois political docility of the masses turned into a petty-bourgeois elemental outburst, and the same masses threw themselves headlong into the arms of the Bolsheviks.

'At that time the S.R. Party was the biggest and the most powerful. But it was a colossus with feet of clay; it was not destined to become a really firm foundation for the new Government. It gave itself up entirely to the Coalition; it gave everything it had.'[4]

Yet it was from this Congress of Soviets that the bourgeoisie received their first intimation of the awful reality of the wrath to come, and of the possibility that they would have to face, not only declining profits and a smaller stake in the country, but liquidation. Lenin, in a speech to the Congress, affirmed that his minority party was ready to assume full power at any time – and this was a warning to other socialists that he was no democrat. He also said that his party would, on assuming power, arrest 'fifty or a hundred of our richest millionaires' and hang them. The speech was greeted with laughter. It sounded impossibly extreme. But there were those who realized that the State itself was in extremis, and a chill wind must have blown through comfortable clubs and drawing-rooms that night.

The concluding act of the First Congress of Soviets was to elect a Central Excom to supersede the Excom born of the February Revolution and the Petrograd Soviet. Lenin and Kerensky were both members, but never attended. The Central Excom was never taken seriously and there was still no keystone to the arch of government. Liberals and

moderate socialists, though now reunited round the same
Cabinet table, exercised different kinds of power, and between them were unable to pursue a consistent policy. It
was on this dangerous tightrope that the mercurial Kerensky
began to perform his political acrobatics. Now Minister of
War, he came to regard himself as a man of destiny, and he
overshadowed, in the public view, all his colleagues, old and
new. Bewildered workers and peasants saw him as the man
who would guide them safely through the capitalist under-
growth towards the socialist paradise; the bourgeoisie saw
him as the man able to bring order out of chaos. Only the
Bolsheviks recognized the essential weakness of his position.

Sukhanov noted that Kerensky, who as Minister of Justice
had worn a dark brown jacket, now, as Minister of War,
had changed it for a light-coloured, elegant officers' tunic.
'His hand had been bothering him all that summer, and in a
black sling gave him the appearance of a wounded hero. I
have no idea what was wrong with Kerensky's hand – it
was a long time since I had talked to him. But it is just so
that he is remembered by hundreds of thousands of soldiers
and officers from Finland to the Black Sea, to whom he
addressed his fiery speeches. Of course a sizeable portion
of the enthusiasm for him was generated by the middle
classes, the officers and the philistines. But even among the
front-line soldiers, in the very trenches, Kerensky had an
enormous success.'[5]

The army Kerensky addressed was in an ambiguous
situation. Towards the end of March an Officers' Union
had been established at Stavka. This had been done partly
for mutual defence against the unruly soldiery and their
regimental soviets, and partly as a means of restoring some
kind of cohesion in an army at war that was receiving con-
tradictory instructions from the Provisional Government and
the Central Soviet. On 3 May, some 300 delegates assembled
in Mogilev's small town theatre for a Congress of Officers.
The High Command did not at first intend to involve itself
in an act likely to be interpreted in Petrograd as politically
provocative. However, word came that the Soviet, with the
approval of Kerensky but not of his liberal colleagues in the
Government, was about to promulgate a new Declaration

of the Rights of Soldiers, carrying the disruptive principles of Order Number One a stage further. This Declaration provided for the free expression of opinion in the army, the abolition of orderlies and the suppression of saluting even on duty.

General Alekseiev, who had been Chief of Staff to the Tsar from 1915, was now Commander-in-Chief. One of the Emperor's last acts before abdicating had been to transfer this post from himself to its former occupant, the Grand Duke Nicholas. The Grand Duke had hastened from the Caucasus, where he was Viceroy, to resume his military duties, but had received a message from Prince Lvov on his arrival at Stavka that the Provisional Government could not allow a Romanov to hold high office. Accordingly he had retired southwards for the second time, to be succeeded by Alekseiev.

The new Commander-in-Chief, feeling that the Declaration of the Rights of Soldiers was the last straw, decided after all to address the Officers' Congress. He declared that, unless the country rallied behind the army and gave it full support, Russia was certain to be conquered by the Germans. The officers, he said, were the only class of the Russian people who had not, since the Revolution, asked anything for themselves. They wanted neither more pay, nor shorter hours, nor less danger. All they asked for was a mandate from the Government to exercise the authority that was necessary to win the war. Within the officers' corps, he said, there was as much diversity of opinion as anywhere else about what form the future Russia should take, but this was beside the point. What was needed for the present was the repeal of the legislation that had made the conduct of the war impossible. The death penalty for desertion must come back, the regimental soviets must be kept in check and political differences must be forgotten. 'Russia is in danger. She stands on the edge of the abyss. A few more shocks and she will crash with all her weight into it.'

The officers applauded, and backed the Commander-in-Chief with an almost unanimous vote. The soldier observers, lolling in the boxes, said nothing; but two days before the Congress ended, General Alekseiev received a telegram from Kerensky, as Minister of War, appointing General Brusilov in his place.

But Kerensky, in giving this sop to the Left, was not to have it all his own way. There was another man of destiny waiting in the wings, and the Congress of Officers, loyally protesting its republicanism, was not the only military organization in the field. A number of spontaneous unions had sprung up – of Knights of St George, of Cossacks, war wounded, escaped prisoners of war, and so forth. These constituted the military wing of a 'Republican Centre' which the big industralists had formed under the auspices of the Siberian Bank to give a broader-based support to Putilov's Society for the Economic Rehabilitation of Russia. Active behind all these scenes was General Kornilov who when he had resigned as Military Governor of Petrograd, had been making only a tactical retreat. Many respectable people came to regard him as the 'man on horseback' who, if the worse came to the worst, might restore law and order under a military dictatorship.

Once again the struggle became, not extra-parliamentary, for since the virtual abdication of the Imperial Duma it had always been that, but extra-governmental. In such circumstances the resort to force, by one side or the other, was inevitable.

The managerial class was now certainly in trouble. The workers had discovered that factory committees could be useful instruments of economic advance. There was little of politics in this at first. The men had no desire to overthrow the capitalist system; they only wanted to get more out of it for themselves. But when their demands were resisted and, as in Tsarist days, local strikes were countered by local lockouts, they seized on the idea of workers' control, or, rather, workers' surveillance, by which representatives of the shop floor were shown a company's accounts before presenting their demands. Such a compromise was accepted by many employers, who knew how to cook their books. Wages rose, even if they scarcely kept pace with inflation. For tactical reasons, the Bolsheviks supported this movement, and thus gained more popularity among the workers.

The new government, concerned about the catastrophic

fall in production, had more advanced ideas. Its Menshevik members had had inserted in the Coalition platform a clause promising that the country's economic breakdown would be countered 'by the inauguration of a more systematic government control of production, transport, exchange and distribution of consumer goods, and, in case of need, by the organization of production'.

This programme sounded revolutionary enough, but, paradoxically, many employers underwrote it. They felt that state control of the economy would serve their interests better than unrest in the factories, since they believed they were strong enough to control the State. They were wrong, because the State was out of all control. The only genuine measure of State socialism the Provisional Government was able to enforce was the wheat monopoly, intended to keep the towns supplied with bread.

The peasants, like the urban workers, were still awaiting the millennium. Armed deserters from the front were flocking home, kicking paying passengers out of the trains; they were eager to play their part in the promised agrarian revolution. Finding that the whole question of land reform had officially been postponed until the meeting of the Constituent Assembly, they were beginning to take the law into their own hands. In the financial confusion more and more estates were passing from the nobility to the new race of kulaks, and it was the latter who faced the first violent challenge. In April 174 agrarian disorders were officially recorded; in May 236; in June 280.

This led to further privation in the towns, though the very rich were still cushioned against it. Inflation was producing a new poor, but there were more speculators than ever. Fabergé continued to ply his exquisite trade, finding new customers. Luxury, as had always been the way in Russia, existed side by side with the direst poverty.

The movement of army deserters was compared by Sukhanov with the great migrations of history. Unkempt soldiers were seen everywhere, sometimes drunk, trampling down the crops in the countryside, spitting out sunflower seeds along the town boulevards (a notorious habit of the Russian lower orders), filling every public place and hectoring every public authority. 'In Russia generally, under the Coalition, in the summer of 1917, there was very little order.'[6]

Nevertheless, behind the shutters of the great houses some lingering reflection of the good old days remained. On 29 June, the Grand Duke Paul gave a dinner party to celebrate his birthday. He wore a dinner jacket with the ribbon of St George, and among the guests were the Grand Duke Boris, released from detention, the Grand Duchess Maria Pavlovna II, Princess and Vladimir Paley and Countess Kleinmichel. A guest described the wines as remarkable, but noticed, as a sign of the times, that two of the servants at table were women. After dinner the little princesses, Irene and Nathalie Paley, acted three playlets in the Empire ballroom. They had been written in French by the children's half-brother Vladimir. One of them, entitled 'Monarchy', was daring enough, since the *dramatis personae* consisted of a king and a young Nihilist dressed all in black.

The Orthodox Church had no positive role to play in this crisis of the nation's affairs. Having been, since the time of Peter the Great, the subservient lackey of the State, it was powerless when the State itself was undergoing a transformation. The notion of 'Holy Russia', which had never been accepted by the liberals, meant nothing without the Tsar, and was rapidly fading from the popular mind. Though the masses still carried out personal religious observances and village communities assisted at the Sunday Liturgy, the parish clergy, as such, exerted little influence, and came to be distrusted as agents of reaction.

The bishops, some of whom were members of the aristocracy, were treated with scant respect. The new procurator of the Holy Synod, N. N. Lvov, removed from office the Metropolitans Pitrim and Makari, on account of their former association with Rasputin, and it was with difficulty that the Provisional Government secured the release of five members of the hierarchy, including the Metropolitan Tikhon, who had been arrested by local soviets.

An all-Russian conference of bishops met in June to consider the new government's proposed charter of the rights and duties of the Church. It declared itself opposed to the socialists' demand for the separation of Church and State, and this question, like so many others, was left in abeyance. But the conference did not offer any kind of spiritual leadership. Freed of imperial restraints, the Russian Church, as an institution, experienced no resurrection.

Paradoxically, it was the Old Believers, to be found chiefly among the native merchant class, who clung longest to the monarchical principle. They had been persecuted at various times in the past, but their innate conservatism was strong enough to attach them by sentiment to the old regime. They had always held aloof from politics, but now, seeking political support from the Right, they found it only in those liberal Cadets they had previously abominated.

There had been little change in the field of education. A teacher delegate at the Congress of Soviets complained that most of the old teachers, inspectors and directors of education, 'many of them former members of the Black Hundreds', were still at their posts, that there had been no change in the curricula and that reactionary textbooks were still being used. The portraits of the Tsar had been removed to the attics, but not destroyed.

The revolutionary euphoria of the poets seemed to evaporate during this baffling period. Men like Alexander Blok and Vladimir Mayakovsky, who in February had declared 'Now everything is possible', were for the time being stricken with much the same inertia as the Government. Censorship had been abolished, but of what use was that when the imperial theatres, reopened under Alexandre Benois, presented the same pieces as before, and when the fall of Tsarism had come to look like a false dawn? Weighed in this particular balance, the revolutionary artists, like the liberals, were found wanting. Their brief period of creative freedom was to come later.

The great Stanislavsky, however, was fascinated by the presence in theatre audiences of working men and women side by side with the bourgeoisie. Their manners were atrocious at first, but good behaviour was soon generated by the seriousness with which they approached the world, quite new to them, of traditional opera, drama and ballet.

'They taught us an important lesson,' Stanislavsky wrote; 'they made us feel an altogether new atmosphere in the auditorium. We began to understand that these people came to the theatre not to be amused but to learn.'

To Lenin the Bolshoi Theatre was 'a piece of pure landlord culture', and he objected to the 'pompous court style of the operas'. Certainly, the spectacle of workers gaping at *Prince Igor* did not in itself represent revolutionary progress in the arts.

The belief that any relationship between art and politics was impossible survived the Revolution for several months in orthodox artistic circles. According to the Soviet historian Nestyev, at meetings of the writers and artists in the spring and summer of 1917, many outstanding representatives of the arts stubbornly asserted art's independence from the influence of the Revolution. The new orthodoxy was later to proclaim the precise opposite.

It was left to Maxim Gorky, literary hero of two worlds and two cultures, to step into the breach and produce a daily paper, the *Novaya Zhizn* ('New Life'), to instigate a flow of fertile revolutionary ideas. But this journal, though it attained a wide circulation, had little real influence.

Gorky had returned to Russia under the amnesty of 1914, and throughout the war had published a review entitled *Letopis* ('Annals') which, within the limits of the Tsarist censorship, had reflected its editor's rather indeterminate form of socialism. He took most of his team of writers with him to start the new venture, but they soon found that making covert attacks on the Autocracy under the nose of the censor had been a different matter from being called upon, in circumstances where comment was suddenly free, to give a lead on questions of the hour in a totally fluid political situation. Gorky's genius was not political, at least in the sense that his beloved enemy or hated friend Lenin would have used that term. Trotsky, for his part, described him as 'the psalm-singer of the Revolution'. His psalms were admonitory, however, and he hit out impartially at almost every political faction in sight, though at first, surprisingly, he expressed a high opinion of the moral and intellectual calibre of the Cadets.

Gorky spent his time among the bourgeois intelligentsia.

All social groups competed for his influence, manufacturers, among them, trying to demonstrate that the workers were criminal idlers who were destroying the national industry, and culture with it.

Stalin, at any rate, was no admirer of Gorky's. During the Petrograd Soviet elections, he wrote in *Proletary*: 'The group "New Life" of electoral list No. 12 is appearing before you. The group expresses the mood of intellectuals who are alienated from life and activity. For this very reason the group oscillates continually between revolution and counter-revolution, war and peace, workers and capitalists, landowners and peasants. To vote for that ambiguous group, to vote for list No. 12, would be to serve the followers of the "Defence of the Fatherland", who in their turn are the servants of counter-revolution.'

In fact, of course, Gorky was the ancient enemy of all forms of exploitation, but his farsightedness, combined with his vanity, precluded him from identifying himself with any particular political group at a time when individual voices could still be heard above the shouting. Consequently he pleased nobody, and fell out with Lenin completely during this period. The bourgeois press condemned him as heartily as did that rising star, the Bolshevik *Pravda*. Supported, presumably, by German money, this publication, once Lenin took control of it, began to exercise an increasing influence on the proletarian movement. Lenin, at any given time, knew exactly what he wanted to say, and said it.

At about this time Dr Manukin, the prison physician at the Fortress of St Peter and St Paul, turned up at the Military Academy to beg that Anna Vyrubova, the Tsaritsa's friend and lady-in-waiting, should be transferred to a prison hospital. The Procurator had agreed, but the Fortress garrison were defying him and refusing to release any of the Tsar's servants. Sukhanov, as a member of the Central Excom, went with the doctor to deal with the matter, largely out of a desire to see the inside of the Russian Bastille, where so many of his friends had been incarcerated. His attitude was that although as citizens the soldiers should work to remove the Coalition Government, as soldiers they were obliged to execute its orders while it was still in office. In any case, he believed, the arbitrary behaviour of individual groups should cease; workers and soldiers could make policy only according to the will of the Soviet.

Sukhanov made his point with the garrison, and Madame Vyrubova ('a pretty young woman, with a simple, typically Russian face', who was on crutches as a result of a railway accident) was duly released. While he was in the fortress, Sukhanov peeped into some of the cells where the Tsarist ministers were being held. 'Protopopov was sound asleep with his back to the door. Stuermer was sitting on a bench holding a small book.'[7]

The last weeks of Prince Lvov's premiership were engulfed in events that shook the effective governance of Russia right out of his hands, and of those of all he represented. There was the army's offensive on the Galician front, its early spectacular successes and its catastrophic failure – the last hopeless venture of the 'Russian steamroller' in the context of the First World War. Simultaneously there were the July Days, when the Bolsheviks, supported by the Kronstadt sailors, made a premature armed attempt to seize power, dominated the centre of Petrograd for a time, and were with difficulty defeated by the Cossacks.

The working class as a whole did not support this rising. It was a spontaneous effort by frustrated extremists who had not yet submitted to strict Bolshevik discipline. Nevertheless, once it had got under way the Party put itself at its head, on the principle that, in any revolutionary situation, the Party must always lead and never follow.

This tactic proved right in the end. True, Lenin went into hiding and Trotsky was arrested, while the Government's publication of a document purporting to show that Lenin was a German agent turned nearly everyone against him in this hour of national defeat at the front. Nevertheless, from the Bolshevik point of view, the abortive insurrection served an excellent purpose. It meant the end of politics for Russia in the accepted western sense of that word.

Prince Lvov had already lost four of his bourgeois ministers, nominally over the question of the autonomy of the Ukraine. After the rising it was clear that the fiction of a coalition government was useless for coping with the dangers that now confronted the nation. The Prince, the last link with pre-revolutionary respectability, resigned, and on 8 July Kerensky became Prime Minister. A strong man was needed at the helm, and Kerensky was believed to be strong.

Thus all pretence of a legitimacy salvaged from the muddled events surrounding the Tsar's abdication was abandoned. Henceforth the Cadets were from time to time brought back into government, but as a bourgeois faction, not through historical right. The struggle was no longer a quasi-constitutional one, between the Soviet and the Provisional Government, or between the liberals and socialists in that Government. All groups and organizations in the nation were now involved, and out for their own. It was the beginning of the class war.

8

Kerensky

The Kerensky period opened with the Bolsheviks in retreat, but from the point of view of the bourgeoisie this was not an unmixed blessing, since it left the rest of the nation more divided than before. It was clear that the struggle was henceforth to be a free-for-all, with not even the most elementary rules of revolutionary legitimacy to control it. To maintain his position, and make some show of governing the country, Kerensky had to defend himself from both Right and Left, by whatever means were at his disposal. He dared not hit too hard in either direction, for fear of causing a violent reaction that would upset the whole frail edifice of the State. He aimed instead at a consenus, where no possibility of a consensus existed. Both sides were mobilizing, and in these circumstances the Bolsheviks, who alone knew precisely what they wanted out of the situation, were destined soon to become once again the most active element in it.

In the aftermath of the July Days, the Cossacks were regarded, by the Petrograd bourgeoisie, as the veritable saviours of civilization. One of their officers, named Grekov, wrote that there were occasions when, upon the entrance into a restaurant of someone in a Cossack uniform, all the guests would stand and greet him with applause. The theatres, the cinemas, and the public gardens instituted a series of benefit evenings for Cossacks wounded in the fighting and for the relatives of the slain. The bureau of the Executive Committee of the Soviet found itself compelled to appoint a commission to participate in the organization of a public funeral for the 'warriors fallen while fulfilling their revolutionary duty in the days of 3–5 July'.

The ceremony began with a mass in St Isaac's Cathedral. The pall-bearers were Rodzianko, Milyukov, Prince Lvov and Kerensky, who marched in procession to the burial-place in the Alexander Nevsky monastery.

Kerensky, in an attempt to placate the Right, threw one life-line back to a now almost forgotten past. He summoned the surviving members of all four of the Tsar's Dumas to meet in an extraordinary assembly and advise on the state of the nation. There could have been no greater anachronism. The leading orators of those past parliaments were precisely the men who were blamed by the Right for having opened the flood-gates of revolution, and by the Left for not carrying that revolution through; they were also the men who had signally failed to influence any of the events since February. Their ghostly voices went unheard, and it was perhaps fortunate that this was so. Their one positive suggestion, that the summoning of the Consitutional Assembly should be postponed until after the war, was aimed at the single fixed star that still shone in the revolutionary firmament.

Since there was nothing to be gained from reviving the corpse of pseudo-constitutionalism, Kerensky turned to the forces that actually existed, to see whether they could be moulded into some semblance of national unity. He hit on the idea of staging, not in excitable Petrograd but in the more patriotic and traditional Moscow, a State conference at which all elements should be represented. Landlords, industrialists, merchants, serving officers, soldiers, workers, peasants, through their now multifarious organizations, were all to send delegates, who would be asked to lend their backing to a government which otherwise had no visible means of support.

But before the State conference could assemble, its constituent elements began to manoeuvre for position in the country at large. A process of polarization began which soon brought the Bolsheviks back into the field. Meanwhile the workers continued their economic strikes, and were much incensed when the Moscow industrailist Ryabushinsky told them they would be brought to their senses by 'the bony hand of hunger'. As for the peasants, they were making life increasingly uncomfortable for the country landlords. The number of agrarian disorders officially recorded in July was 325.

On the opposing side, the upper bourgeoisie, realizing that political action through the Cadet Party was no longer effective, and that it scarcely mattered whether the Cadets were in or out of government, began to rally their forces in a more conspiratorial manner. In Petrograd, Putilov's Society for the Economic Rehabilitation of Russia improved its relations with the more militant Republican Centre, while in Moscow the All-Russian Union of Trade and Industry, which had been formed in the last desperate days of Tsardom, made discreet contacts with the officers' organizations, and gained the support of the All-Russian Landowners' Congress.

The sinister General Kornilov was privy to these moves. On 16 July he attended a meeting in the Northern Hotel, Moscow, where he met Kerensky, the Cadets V. D. Nabokov and N. M. Kishkin, and two leading industrialists, Kutler, from Petrograd, and Tretyakov, from Moscow. On the same day Kerensky presided over a conference of senior generals, and Trotsky, recording their names – Brusilov, Alexeiev, Ruzsky, Denikin – said they 'sounded like the last echo of an epoch that was disappearing into the abyss'. For four months, he pointed out, 'these high generals had regarded themselves as half dead'.[1] But the important outcome of the meeting was that next day Kornilov was appointed Supreme Commander-in-Chief, in place of Brusilov.

In advance of the State Conference the Union of Trade and Industry organized a 'Conference of Public Men' in Moscow. It was attended by the top generals Brusilov, Kaledin and Yudenich, and by representatives of the officers' associations. The conference sent a telegram of support to Kornilov, who at that time was urging Kerensky to let him impose military discipline on the railways and in the factories and take more positive action against the land seizures. Meanwhile in Petrograd a Conference of the League of Knights of St George declared that if Kornilov were removed from office, as some of the socialists were demanding, they would join in a united rebellion with the Cossacks.

The Orthodox Church was also brought into play. Following the conference of bishops an All-Russian Church Council met in Moscow for the first time in two centuries. Its ostensible object was the 'revolutionary' one of freeing the ecclesiastical establishment from bureaucratic control, but the laymen who arranged the agenda – liberals like Rodzianko, Prince Trubetskoy and Count Olsufiev – were more concerned with using the mystique of religion in defence of law and order. At the opening ceremony in the Uspensky Cathedral in the Kremlin, Russia's Westminster Abbey, a Social-Revolutionary, Rudner, the new mayor, declared: 'So long as the Russian people shall live, the Christian faith will burn in its soul.'

The State Conference itself, which met on 12 August, was the last public occasion on which the ancient trappings of Holy Russia were brought out, in opposition to the slogans and red banners of socialism. Kerensky and Kornilov were vying for public support, like two rival claimants to Nicholas's vacant throne.

Kornilov had a great reception at the railway station, where officers and their ladies, frock-coated leaders of the city's business community and robed bishops and clergy from the Church Council were drawn up to welcome him. The ex-Tsar himself would have felt at home on an occasion such as this. As Trotsky had described it, the Tekintsi bodyguard, all Muslims, leapt from the approaching train in their long, bright red coats, with their naked curved swords, and drew up in two files on the platform. Ecstatic ladies covered the hero with flowers as he reviewed the bodyguard and the deputations. Patriotic sobbings were heard. Morozova, a millionaire merchant's wife, went down on her knees. Officers carried Kornilov out to the people on their shoulders.

Meanwhile Kerensky, in his capacity of rival tribune and Minister of War, was reviewing a parade of the Moscow garrison in another part of the city. This might have been considered more realistic, but Kornilov was playing for higher stakes. On the way from the station he stopped, like a Tsar about to be crowned, at the Shrine of the Iberian Virgin, and knelt in prayer.

The Bolsheviks boycotted the State Conference. What is more, they demonstrated their renewed influence over the workers by instigating a lightning general strike in Moscow, causing the delegates to walk to the Bolshoi Theatre where the meeting was held and making it difficult for them to find anything to eat.

In the lime-lit atmosphere of the theatre Kerensky appeared to score over his rival. Kornilov received a standing ovation from the well-dressed part of the house when he declared that the Germans were at the gates of Riga while the Russian army had been 'turned into a crazy mob trembling for its own life'; but his own soldiers and the socialist delegates remained firmly in their seats. Kerensky fared better. When, after a melodramatic speech calling for revolutionary unity, he sank exhausted into the arms of his aides-de-camp, the whole audience applauded him. As Sir Robert Bruce Lockhart, the British Consul, described it: 'A millionaire's wife threw her pearl necklace on to the stage. Every woman present followed her example, and a hail of jewellery descended from every tier of the huge house.'

This was the last momentary demonstration of unity between the propertied classes of Russia and the non-Bolshevik part of the proletariat. The two distinct 'moderate' aims, the one for the establishment of a parliamentary democracy, the other for a social revolution proceeding by safe and easy stages, were henceforth to be pursued separately, and by increasingly immoderate means. The State Conference came and went, leaving Kerensky at the helm and as helpless as before.

Supreme Commander Kornilov left Moscow in disgust, and began his preparations to march on Petrograd and take over the government. The 'Kornilov Affair' was the only attempt by the Right, before Russia fell apart territorially and the civil war broke out, to regain control of the State by force of arms. It failed because the bulk of the demoralized army would not play. Kornilov had been admired by the troops as an attractive rough diamond, as a man who had risen from the Cossack ranks against the imperial system and as a relatively successful wartime general. But few soldiers wanted him as a dictator, who would put the revolution into reverse, especially after his attempts to restore a measure of pre-revolutionary discipline and his open flirtation with the propertied classes.

Historians differ as to the extent to which, when it came to the point, Kornilov's attempted coup was backed by the natural leaders of the bourgeoisie. Putilov and a part of his Society for the Economic Rehabilitation of Russia are known to have given him financial support, but Tretyakov, leader of the Moscow industrialists, stood aside. Not all the generals were implicated, and certainly not all the members of the officers' associations. Moreover, the Cossack regiments, whose conservatism sprung from their desire to preserve their special privileges, showed themselves much less eager to overthrow the Provisional Government in August than to protect it from the Bolsheviks in July.

Kerensky's own role in the affair was equivocal. He too must have been disappointed at the failure of the State Conference to build a bridge between the two sections of society, and he seems to have contemplated at first a Machiavellian alliance with Kornilov. But to cover his Left flank he put two idle grand dukes, Michael and Paul, under house arrest for a time, and let it be known that other members of the old regime were under observation. This was irrelevant to the real situation, as Trotsky satirically pointed out.

'Former officials, aides-de-camp, ladies-in-waiting, Black Hundred courtiers, witch doctors, monks, ballerinas, whispering here and there in the back yards. That was a thing of no consequence whatever. The victory of the bourgeoisie could only come in the form of a military dictatorship. The question of monarchy could only arise at some future stage, and then too on the basis of a bourgeois counter-revolution, not of Rasputin's ladies-in-waiting. The real thing was the struggle of the bourgeoisie against the people under the banner of Kornilov. Seeking an alliance with this camp,

Kerensky was all the more willing to screen himself from the suspicions of the Left with a fictitious arrest of grand dukes.'[2]

However, when on 25 August Kornilov actually began to move his troops, Kerensky suddenly realized the danger of his personal position. He then flung the helm right over, and threw himself into the arms of the Left. The Bolsheviks were quite willing to reactivate their Red Guards, though against Kornilov rather than in favour of Kerensky. They received their share of arms, which they never afterwards surrendered. This, though few suspected it at the time, was a turning-point in the history not only of Russia but of the world.

The melting away of Kornilov's assault force against Petrograd, including the Cossack Savage Division, proved that the 'man on horseback' had no horse. It also proved that the man in the White Palace, sleeping in the Tsar's four-poster bed, was no new Tsar. Once again it was the Petrograd Soviet, aided this time by the Bolsheviks, who took the lead; it organized its own Military Committee for the defence of the capital.

Though Kerensky's rightist rival was now under arrest, his own position was weaker than ever. He was no longer the darling of the Right, and he had certainly not ingratiated himself with the Left. For this reason he felt it necessary to assume the trappings of personal power. He dismissed his political cabinet, declared himself to be Generalissimo of the armed forces, and formed a 'Directorate' of four, consisting of Tereshchenko, who had succeeded Milyukov as Foreign Minister, the Menshevik Nikitin, and two mildly left-wing officers, General Verkhovsky, a former page of the Dowager Empress, who was released from prison for the purpose, and Admiral Verderevsky.

As a sop to the Left, this body, completely illegal by any standards, did not wait for the coming Constituent Assembly but declared Russia to be a republic. True, there were now few open monarchists left in Russia, but this formal announcement of the country's status by a dictator and his henchmen, without reference to any kind of elected body, was the final indication that the seat of authority in the State was no longer a matter of constitutional theory, 'revolutionary' or otherwise. It was now 'the simple plan, that they should take who have the power, and they should keep who can'.

Fernand Grenard wrote:

'At the critical hour the upper classes of Russia continued with their vague and illogical policy. They might have rallied all their forces, which were still great at that time, to the assistance of the temporary defenders of the State. They might have helped the Provisional Government to combat the terrible danger and the threat of disaster, plunder and massacre. They refrained from doing so, the majority of the ruling classes putting their hopes in a double blow: to have Kerensky killed by the Bolsheviks – who were supposed to be too weak to stand on their own – so as to beat the victors themselves on the day after their victory.'[3]

History was moving fast. On 1 August the former symbol of Russia's nationhood, with his wife, heir and daughters, had already left his great palace outside Petrograd, under guard, for Siberia. Few of those who had once been his subjects spared him a thought.

9

The Abyss

When, at the beginning of September, Sukhanov went to the Winter Palace to protest against the temporary suppression of Gorky's *New Life*, he found the rooms noisy, disorderly and faded. Nevertheless some of the appurtenances of former days were still to be seen. 'Inscrutable, exquisitely polite cadet sentries. Long-forgotten, sulky, arrogantly obsequious *ancien-régime* functionaries' faces. Glossy, brilliant officers slithering over the dubious parquet.'[1]

But at the Smolny Institute, which had now become the seat of the Soviets, there was a different scene. The Savage Division had arrived to make a confession of guilt to the Soviet. 'The Bureau was packed tight with Caucasian greatcoats, fur caps, felt cloaks, galoons, daggers, glossy black moustaches, astounded prawn-like eyes and the smell of horses. This was the *élite*, the cream, headed by "native" officers – in all perhaps 500 men. Cap in hand, they professed their loyalty to the Revolution, and explained that "a misunderstanding had taken place, dissipated by the simple establishment of the truth".'[2]

The Cossacks were to play no further part in the unfolding of events, outside their home ground. The last support of the bourgeoisie was withdrawn, and there was no more applause for a Cossack officer when he entered a fashionable restaurant.

Nevertheless, in spite of everything that had happened since February, Russia, in the last two months of the Provisional Government's regime, was still a capitalist country. In theory, and to a large extent in practice, the old possessing classes were still the possessors. No official decree had been promulgated that infringed the sacred right of private property. The shape of the future was to depend on the decisions of the Constituent Assembly, due to meet in December, and, though the bourgeoisie dreaded what might come of it and had already despaired of the Cadet Party as the defenders of their interests, they had not altogether abandoned the hope that the hard facts of economic life, as they understood them, would soon restore Russian society to a condition in which they would again enjoy the full privileges of wealth. The failure of Kornilov's military coup had robbed them of any hope of directly imposing their will on the machinery of State, and they had begun to look further afield for salvation – even to the victory, which now seemed eminently possible, of the Kaiser's armies. Pure patriotism ceased, in Russia, to be an upper-class virtue.

In this twilit period the possession of property was certainly not the unmixed blessing it had formerly been. Landlords, in many parts of the country, were losing their rents and their demesnes, being chased out of their manor houses, and even murdered. Managers of factories were having to share their authority with the shop floor and were dealing with innumerable strikes. No wealthy Russian's home was now his castle; arbitrary searches and requisitions could happen any day or night. The emigration of those who had substantial funds abroad had already begun.

In October, Princess Urossov arrived in Petrograd from Lapotkovo, her estate at Tula. The peasants had burned and pillaged everything. The old Princess was ill, and they had dragged her out of bed and left her for several hours in the courtyard, shivering with fever and cold. Some Austrian prisoners of war had saved her by taking her to the railway station. The peasants had dug up the body of her son, who had been killed at the beginning of the war, to see if they could find any jewellery or medals on it; they left it half out of the grave, still recognizable.

Trotsky described the plight of the landlords at this time in his inimitable way. They were, he said, awaiting the outcome of events as a hopelessly rich man awaits death.

'Autumn with *mujiks* is the time for politics. The fields are reaped, illusions are scattered, patience is exhausted. Time to finish things up! The movement now overflows its banks, invades all districts, wipes out local peculiarities, draws in all the strata of the villages, washes away all considerations of law and prudence, becomes aggressive, fierce, furious, a raging thing, arms itself with steel and fire, revolvers and hand-grenades, demolishes and burns up the manorial dwellings, drives out the landlords, cleanses the earth and in some places waters it with blood.

'Gone are the nests of gentility celebrated by Pushkin, Turgeniev and Tolstoy. The old Russia has gone up in smoke. The liberal press is a collection of groans and outcries about the destruction of "English" gardens, of paintings from the brushes of serfs, of patrimonial libraries, the parthenons of Tombov, the riding horses, the ancient engravings, the breeding bulls. Bourgeois historians have tried to put the responsibility upon the Bolsheviks for the "vandalism" of the peasant's mode of settling accounts with the "culture" of his lords. In reality the Russian *mujik* was completing a business entered upon many centuries before the Bolsheviks appeared in the world. He was fulfilling his progressive task with the only means at his disposal.'[3]

In September and early October serious agrarian disturbances, often involving the destruction of crops as well as manor houses, were reported from the regions of Tombov, Taganrog, Kishinev, Odessa, Zhitomir, Voronezh, Chernigov, Penza and Nizhny-Novgorod. In agitations against the wheat monopoly two food administrators were killed. Pillaging and the destruction of private property occurred in the towns of Kharkov, Simferopol, Astrakhan, Saratov, Ekaterinburg, Tiflis and Tashkent. At Rostov-on-Don a member of the municipal duma was thrown down the stairs of the city hall; at Spassk, Count Grabbe lost his valuable library.

Nevertheless, disorders do not in themselves amount to a

social revolution, and a way of life is not easily abandoned. It is even pursued with greater intensity when the immediate future is in doubt. Eat, drink and be merry, for tomorrow we die.

This phenomenon was noted with exasperation by the American sympathizer with the Bolsheviks, John Reed, in his classic piece of eye-witness history *Ten Days that Shook the World*. He noted that at the Troitsky Farce Theatre in Petrograd a burlesque called *Sins of the Tsar* was interrupted by a group of monarchists, who threatened to lynch the actors for 'insulting the Emperor'.

'Of course all the theatres were going every night, including Sundays. Karsavina appeared in a new ballet at the Mariinsky, all dance-loving Russia coming to see her. Chaliapin was singing. At the Alexandrinsky they were reviving Meyerhold's production of Tolstoy's *Death of Ivan the Terrible*; and at that performance I remember noticing a student of the Imperial School of Pages, in his dress uniform, who stood up correctly between the acts and faced the empty imperial box, with its eagles all erased.'[4]

This was indeed a defiant gesture, recalling the etiquette of pre-revolutionary days, which demanded that officers present at the theatre should stand during the intervals facing the imperial box even when it was empty, in case Their Majesties should unexpectedly appear.

Although the Hermitage and other art galleries had been evacuated to Moscow, there were weekly exhibitions of paintings in Petrograd. According to Reed, 'hordes of the female intelligentsia went to hear lectures on Art, Literature, and the Easy Philosophies. It was a particularly active season for Theosophists. And the Salvation Army, admitted to Russia for the first time in history, plastered the walls with announcements of gospel meetings, which amused and astounded Russian audiences.

'As in all such times, the petty conventional life of the city went on, ignoring the Revolution as much as possible. The poets made verses – but not about the Revolution. The realistic painters painted scenes from medieval Russian history – anything but the Revolution. Young ladies from the provinces came up to the capital to learn French and cultivate their voices, and the gay young beautiful officers wore their gold-trimmed crimson *bashliki* and their elaborate Caucasian swords around the hotel lobbies. The ladies of the minor bureaucratic set took tea with each other in the afternoon, carrying each her little gold or silver or jewelled sugar-box, and half a loaf of bread in her muff, and wished that the Tsar were back, or that the Germans would come, or anything that would solve the servant problem. The daughter of a friend of mine came home one afternoon in hysterics because the woman street-car conductor had called her "Comrade!"....[5]

'Peter the Great's *Tabel o Rangov* – Table of Ranks – which he riveted upon Russia with an iron hand, still held sway. Almost everybody from the schoolboy up wore his prescribed uniform, with the insignia of the Emperor on button and shoulder-strap. Along about five o'clock in the afternoon the streets were full of subdued old gentlemen in uniform, with portfolios, going home from work in the huge, barrack-like Ministries or Government institutions, calculating perhaps how great a mortality among their superiors would advance them to the coveted *chin* (rank) of Collegiate Assessor, or Privy Councillor, with the prospect of retirement on a comfortable pension, and possibly the Cross of St Anne.

'There is the story of Senator Sokolov, who in full tide of Revolution came to a meeting of the Senate one day in civilian clothes, and was not admitted because he did not wear the prescribed livery of the Tsar's service!

'It was against this background of a whole nation in ferment and disintegration that the pageant of the Rising of the Russian Masses unrolled.'[6]

There was never, in fact, any 'rising of the Russian masses', but only a skilfully organized *coup d'état*. Nevertheless, the success of this depended on a notable advance of the Bolsheviks' influence on proletarian affairs. In August they won a majority vote in the Petrograd Soviet, and one by one the big city soviets followed suit – Moscow, Kiev, Odessa. It now looked as though, when the Second All-Russian Congress of Soviets met in November, it would have a Bolshevik majority.

The moderate socialists who still controlled the permanent

Central Executive Committee of the Congress took fright at this. They urged Kerensky to call a 'Democratic Conference' that could offer some kind of institutional resistance to the Bolshevik threat. He suggested a miniature replica of the abortive State Conference, which should include all the 'live forces' in the nation, by which he meant bankers, industrialists and landlords, and even representatives of the now discredited Cadet Party. This was too much for the Central Excom, but it put forward a socialist list that would ensure a non-Bolshevik majority. Kerensky threatened to resign if the bourgeoisie were not represented, and he had his way. The outcome was a bourgeois-dominated ministry and a nominated 'Pre-Parliament' in which, under the guise of non-party 'public men', the propertied classes had a greater proportion of seats than they could have hoped for.

Thus, at the end of Russia's life as a capitalist State, there was a kind of coalition government again. But it was one that occupied a very narrow sector of the political spectrum, and it was held together only by fear. It tried in vain to prevent the summoning of the full Congress of Soviets, arguing that this was unnecessary on the eve of the election of a Constituent Assembly. 'All power to the Soviets' became once again a Bolshevik slogan, and it proved to be irresistible.

When we think of what *Izvestia* came to stand for after the October Revolution, it is odd to read that on 28 September it was urging, in the most complacent language of liberal democracy, that the Soviets, having served their purpose, should retire from the political scene:

'At last a truly democratic government born of the will of all classes of the Russian people, the first rough form of the future liberal parliamentary regime, has been formed. Ahead of us is the Constituent Assembly, which will solve all questions of fundamental law and whose composition will be essentially democratic. The function of the Soviets is at an end, and the time is approaching when they must retire, with the rest of the revolutionary machinery, from the stage of a free and victorious people, whose weapons shall hereafter be the peaceful ones of political action.'

This was not the impression that M. Philips Price, correspondent of the *Manchester Guardian*, received when he made an enterprising September visit to the provinces. He travelled in the first-class saloon of a Volga steamer, where there was a deceptive calm.

'How quiet and respectable it was!', he reported, 'so conscious of its superiority over the "rabble" of the lower deck.' But he overheard a revealing conversation:

' "I say there is no hope for Russia till we have a dictator who can discipline these dogs and stop all this anarchy", said a man in a general's uniform to his neighbour, a well-dressed civilian. They were sitting at a mahogany table, taking coffee and rolls.

' "Oh yes, that's quite true", said the civilian. "Before the Revolution the peasants on our estate used to work well, but of course you always had to be there with the threat of force to drive them. I suppose it's just the same with the soldiers in the army."

' "Yes, yes; they must have someone to rule over them. They flounder about in times like these, and don't know how to act. They are a dark and ignorant lot. Only a strong man can deal with them. Kerensky is a well-meaning creature, but weak. Alexeiev and Kornilov are the only people for Russia now, and I think the people would welcome them with open arms. I told that the other day to the secretary of the French Embassy in Petrograd." '[7]

At that point, wrote Price, a gorgeous lady with coloured eyelashes and painted lips came up to the general, to show him some jewels. ' "I bought them in Moscow for 600 roubles apiece. Before the war they were 50 roubles each. I got them in a little shop in the Arbat. Alschwang's is no good now, except for dinner. I got magnificent caviar there last week." '[8]

In Samara Price entered quite a different world. He visited the bureau of the local Soviet of Peasants' Deputies, housed in the former Tsarist Governor's house.

'In talking of the agrarian problem, they adopted a somewhat apologetic tone, as if something were happening on the land for which they were not responsible. "They accuse us in Petrograd of being robbers and destroying the landlords' properties", said one of the deputies, "but the fact is we have done everything to restrain the peasants. At the last conference of the Social Revolutionary Party for the province we laid down that the land committees should temporarily take over the estates on public account." '9

A young peasant soldier offered to take Price to his home village, Grachefka, on the railway to Central Asia.

'It was Sunday, and about midday, after Mass in the village church, the village Soviet was meeting by the common barn on the village green.

'The scene was more like a village fair than a public gathering at which business was to be transacted. It seemed a picturesque muddle with a strong Asiatic tinge in it. Bearded patriarchs in fur caps were gathered in one group and were holding forth on the price of corn; a travelling Tartar was squatting on the ground offering Persian carpets for sale; some women in picturesque peasant costumes were complaining about the absence of sugar in the village; a group of peasants in sheepskins were discussing the Kornilov rebellion; gypsies were selling furs; soldiers back on leave were relating stories of life at the front. Mangy dogs were walking in and out of the crowd; a ragged beggar pushed his way into a company of village worthies who were discussing the Social-Revolutionary Party's new directions for the land committees and asked for alms "in the name of the Mother of God". The village priest, with his sonorous voice, began to attract a crowd round him and appealed for subscriptions in support of the parish church school. "Eh, little Father," said someone, "you want to show us the way up there; but we have had a revolution, and are content to wait down here for a while yet."

'The meeting eventually agreed that the regulations of the Soviet of Peasants' Deputies be disregarded, and that the local landlord's demesne and latifundium be annexed to the commune. The chief thing in their minds was to get the land into their own hands and so face the authorities with a *fait accompli*. Then it would be possible to prevent the land-hungry proletarians of Petrograd and Moscow from coming and claiming a share, and counter-revolutionary generals from returning the land to the landlords. In this decision everyone seemed united.

'The commune was still a happy family this Sunday afternoon. The classes of rich, poor and middle peasant had already appeared, but they still had a common object, the liquidation of the last relics of feudalism.'[10]

Two days later Price called on the man who until recently had been the local landlord. The manor house was situated in a wide expanse of beautiful black-earth steppe. Groves of poplars surrounded it. The home farm had only 20 acres attached to it now – all that was left of a 3,000-dessiatine (8,100 acres) estate. The rest had been annexed by the commune in spite of the threats of the Provisional Government in Petrograd.

'I walked through the shrubbery up to the wooden, two-storey house, plastered with stucco. Grass was growing on the roof, and in the dilapidated greenhouse a cow was finishing off what remained of the ferns. An old servant answered the bell and took the "English reporter" to the squire, who was in his study packing up to go away the next day. He was an ex-soldier, a general, who had been educated in that most aristocratic of institutions in Tsarist Petrograd, the Corps of Pages, had served in the Life Guards, and had been through the Russo-Turkish war with the old Grand Duke Nicholas.

' "I am going to turn my back on this place for good," he said, "because I hear that the commune has passed a resolution that all spare rooms in this house are to be used for a new school. I can find rest in the Crimea, unless this anarchy has broken out there. If no parts of Russia remain safe, I shall have to ask the hospitality of your country." He used not to like Englishmen, he said, because Lord Beaconsfield had robbed Russia of the fruits of Plevna and the Shipka Pass, and he, as a young lieutenant, had taken part in those battles; but he did not seem to have any diffidence about accepting the hospitality of his former national enemies in retiring from his struggle with the much more dangerous class enemy at home. He sighed as he quoted the lines of Pushkin's poem *The Robber Brothers*: "We live without power or law; like flocks of ravens they come and sweep over the land."

' "Everything used to be quiet and orderly here, and my

peasants were contented. I gave them seed-corn, and even bought them manure when they were in difficulties. Nobody wanted any change. But agitators have come from the town and stirred the peasants up. I blame the Cadets for having allowed all this talk about 'democracy' to get about. They ought to have stopped this rabble long ago. Now it is too late."

'One had a pang at the complete disappearance of this type, for on the bookshelf opposite me lay a collection of poems written in his youthful days by the occupant of this manor. They were fruits of that leisure that had given many gems of art, literature and music to the world.'[11]

On the following Sunday Price visited the Holy Trinity monastery, twenty versts to the south. Its abbot was supposed to be a very holy man, and, as a disciple of the notorious Iliodor, had acquired a reputation for working miracles. He had discovered that it was a paying thing to be holy. Land had been given him by local squires.

'I was hoping to have an interview with this important personage, but on my arrival I was told he had left some days ago. The Revolution had penetrated into the sacred precincts of the monastery; the monks had gone on strike and had turned out the abbot, who had put them on short commons while selling produce to the towns at speculative prices. Now the "Soviet of Monastic Deputies" had turned over to the neighbouring commune all land they could not work, and worked the rest on a communal basis.'[12]

The internal ferment in the autumn of 1917 was heightened by the undeniable fact that the mighty Russian empire, as it had been known and feared for centuries, was falling apart. In theory both the liberals and the socialists had been in favour of autonomy for the subject nationalities, but, when the Tsarist grip on them was loosened, it was found, in nearly every case, that reactionary elements took the lead in the various liberation movements. Thus the Finnish Senate declined to lend money to the Provisional Government and demanded the withdrawal of Russian troops. The Rada, or parliament, at Kiev claimed as Ukrainian all the richest farmlands in southern Russia, formed its own army with the help of disgruntled Russian officers, and began to look to the advancing Germans for support. General Kaledin, the aristocratic Ataman of Don Cossacks, had been dismissed by the Provisional Government for complicity in the Kornilov Affair, but the Cossack armies insisted that he be reinstated.

Thus was drawn in outline the map of the coming civil war. By offering the bourgeoisie of Great Russia a new hope based on territory, this development weakened their resolve to maintain their position in Petrograd and Moscow. It turned them into potential traitors, like the *émigrés* of the French Revolution, looking for outside help, whether from the Germans or, later, from the victorious Allies. Since the Bolsheviks were potential traitors too, being willing, pending the outbreak of world revolution, to make peace at any price with the Germans, a country that was destined half a century later to become a super-power ceased for the time being to exist as a force in world politics.

Yet, as John Reed has reminded us, the gay life of Petrograd continued to the end. 'Gambling clubs functioned hectically from dusk to dawn, with champagne flowing and stakes of twenty thousand roubles. In the centre of the city at night prostitutes in jewels and expensive furs walked up and down, crowding the cafés.'[13]

Count Lucien de Robien, dining at Contant's restaurant, found Prince and Princess Radziwill there, as well as Mme de Derfelden, back from the Caucasus, 'with her escort of horse-guards'. Gulesko was performing, 'making a hellish noise, rolling the whites of his eyes, and twisting himself into every kind of contortion while playing *Allah Verdi* or the *March of the Hussars* in every octave and with every known variation. While dining in this elegant circle I thought of Etienne de Beaumont's apt observation when, during the early days of the revolution, he pointed out to me that the most important events seem like mere incidents to the people who live through them, and that one continues to live one's life, attaching importance to minor worries and preoccupied with small details.'[14]

'All is changed,' wrote Trotsky, echoing John Reed, 'and yet all remains as before. The Revolution has shaken the country, deepened the split, frightened some, embittered others, but has not yet wiped out a thing or replaced it. Imperial St Petersburg seems drowned in a sleepy lethargy rather than dead. The Revolution has stuck little red flags in the hands of the cast-iron monuments of the monarchy. Great red streamers are hanging down the fronts of the government buildings. But the palaces, the ministries, the headquarters, seem to be living a life entirely apart from those red banners, tolerably faded, moreover, by the autumn rains. The two-headed eagles with the sceptre of empire have been torn down where possible, but oftener draped or hastily painted over. They seem to be lurking there. All the old Russia is lurking, its jaws set in rage. . . . The Tsarist generals remain generals, the Senators senatorialize, the privy councillors defend their dignity. . . . Schoolboys are still studying the old textbooks, functionaries drawing up the same useless papers, poets scribbling the verses that nobody reads, nurses telling the fairy-tales about Ivan Tsarevitch. . . . The remnants of the old banquet are still very plentiful and everything can be had for big money. The Guards officers still click their spurs accurately and go after adventures. Wild parties are in progress in the private dining-rooms of expensive restaurants.'[15]

But on Sunday, 21 October Colonel Caillaut, of the French Embassy, escorted the British Ambassadress, Lady Georgina Buchanan, to the ballet. Though they enjoyed *Paquita* they were puzzled at seeing no one they knew in the audience. The Ambassador's liberal friends had at last been alerted to the imminent danger in which they stood. Four days later the Provisional Government collapsed as suddenly as the Autocracy had done eight months before, and Russia's brief and confused move towards parliamentary democracy was over.

10

October 1917

The insurrection in Petrograd that transformed the personal life of every citizen of Russia and profoundly affected the destiny of mankind was carried out with consummate skill. It involved the preliminary capture by Red Guards of key installations in the city, such as the railway stations, the power station, the telephone exchange and the bridges across the Neva; then a limited use of force against the seat of government in the Winter Palace, timed precisely to make possible the establishment of a moral ascendancy over the Second All-Russian Congress of Soviets, then gathering; and it also involved seizing the momentum to apply at once, in conditions of appalling difficulty, the basic principles of Communist rule. 'We shall now proceed to construct the socialist order', said Lenin on the second day, 26 October – and so it was.

The October Revolution differed from its predecessor in February in two important respects. Those who attacked the *status quo* knew what they wanted; and those who defended it were not mere tyrants but men who had spent the last eight months forming congresses of all kinds and attending meetings at which the future of Russian society had been freely and endlessly discussed. Thus, although October in a narrow sense was a superbly planned *coup d'état* involving the death of about twenty persons, on another plane it was a tremendous battle of ideas.

The propertied classes were the silent victims of this struggle. They did not react to it in any decisive way. They had become inured to violence, disorders and government changes at the top, and they were resigned to the social and economic developments implicit in their fitful alliance with the moderate socialists. They greatly under-estimated the power of a small group of fanatics to turn their world upside down. In February they had recognized a tornado, and, cowering, had waited for it to blow itself out. In October they went about their business as usual.

On the day the Provisional Government was overthrown the shops were open, the trams ran and the cinemas were crowded. One of the most significant events in the history of mankind took place almost unnoticed. This astonished John Reed. 'All the complex routine of common life – humdrum even in wartime – proceeded as usual. Nothing is so astounding as the vitality of the social organism – how it persists in feeding itself, clothing itself, amusing itself, in the face of the worst calamities.'[1]

The physical force that Kerensky could rely on for the defence of his regime had turned out to be as small as the forces loyal to the Tsar. When he discovered that the army, including the Cossacks, was neutral, he could turn only to the *yunkers*, officer-cadets at the local Sandhursts who, though now officially drawn from all classes, were in the nature of things mostly boys of good family, and to the romantic 'Women's Brigade' which he had formed as a symbol of determined resistance to the German invaders. These pathetic groups played a brave but ineffectual part in the defence of the Winter Palace. In Moscow the *yunkers* did rather better, managing to hold the Kremlin for several days.

For the Kerensky regime to survive, more was needed than the foolhardy efforts of these children. But no one who could claim to represent the nation at large came to the rescue of the political institutions that the Minister-President had devised as the basis of his power. He himself had vanished from the capital, in the vain hope of persuading loyal troops to march against it. His ministers were arrested after the shelling of the Winter Palace by the cruiser *Aurora* and its invasion by the mob. A handful of soldiers was enough to put paid to the Pre-Parliament.

It was left to the Petrograd city duma to make the only official *démarche* against the insurrection. On 25 October, at 1.30 a.m., it decided by 62 votes to 18 to march on the Winter Palace and 'die with the Provisional Government'. Led by Mayor Schreider, who carried a lantern in one hand and an umbrella in the other, the sad little procession sallied forth into the night on its mission to save Russia. After walking three blocks it was turned back by a chance patrol of Red Guards.

In the confusion that followed, the moderate socialists joined briefly with the bourgeoisie to form a 'Committee for the Salvation of the Fatherland and the Revolution'. Even in those desperate days this *ad hoc* body attracted to itself some of the prestige of the well-ordered past. John Reed has described their meetings in the Alexander Hall.

'The gold and red epaulettes of the officers were conspicuous, the familiar faces of the Menshevik and Socialist Revolutionist intellectuals, the hard eyes and bulky magnificence of bankers and diplomats, officials of the old regime and well-dressed women.

'The telephone girls were testifying. Girl after girl came to the tribune – over-dressed, fashion-aping little girls, with pinched faces and leaky shoes. Girl after girl, flushing with pleasure at the applause of the "nice" people of Petrograd, of the officers, the rich, the great names of politics – girl after girl, to narrate her sufferings at the hands of the proletariat and to proclaim her loyalty to all that was old-fashioned and powerful.'[2]

Nothing came of these deliberations, though two days after the Provisional Government had fallen a Conference of Businessmen in Moscow was still making the most reactionary demands. In general the upper classes were overtaken by a kind of paralysis, during which they expected the Bolsheviks to throw in their hand any day out of the sheer impossibility of governing on such a slender basis of power. But the new government was extending that basis hourly, and concentrating on winning over the doubtful soviets, of both workers and peasants.

Yet, underground, a remnant of the Provisional Government still existed. It consisted of under-secretaries or junior ministers who, not having been in the Winter Palace at the time of its capture, had so far escaped arrest. Their leader was the intrepid Countess Sophia Panina, former Under-Secretary for Education, who presided over secret meetings of her colleagues in her Petrograd apartment nearly every day between 25 October and 3 November. Using an authority which the banks still recognized, they managed to transfer Government funds abroad.

Much more significant in the losing struggle against Bolshevik power was the Central Strike Committee of Government Institutions. It was this body that nearly reversed the Bolshevik coup by withdrawing the labour of that conservative-minded bureaucracy upon which Russia even now – and, indeed, especially now – depended. For several weeks the new Council of People's Commissars was unable to make use of State funds, of the telegraphs, or, in fact, of any part of the Government machine.

There were two views in this Strike Committee. Vladimir Korostovetz, of the Ministry of Foreign Affairs, recorded that members of departments that did not come into direct contact with the public favoured a stoppage of all State services, which would have affected electricity, water and transport. But officials of the Finance Ministry, the State Savings Banks and the Post Office, many of whom lived above their offices, were afraid that were they to cease work altogether the Bolsheviks would be able to whip up public resentment against them and have them lynched. They obtained the permission of the Strike Committee to carry on with their work, but as independently as possible of the new Government.

The partial strike was not without effect. The Central Strike Committee had various meetings with the Government, and a kind of armistice was called pending the meeting of the Constituent Assembly. Thus it was agreed that the State Bank should be managed by four directors without the participation either of the Bolsheviks or of the Strike Committee, but that if the Assembly proved to have a Bolshevik majority one of the directors should cede his place to a Bolshevik pending a new settlement. Lenin, who by that time had no intention of submitting to the Constituent Assembly, must have agreed to this with his tongue in his cheek, but that he did so at all indicates that in the immediate aftermath of the October Revolution he was far from being master in his own house.

The bourgeois civil servants failed to rally to their side the workers in Government service. Potel, the postal workers' union, and Vikshel, that of the railway workers, conducted independent negotiations with the new Government. Thus the strike was doomed to failure from the first, though it certainly gave the Bolsheviks some uncomfortable moments.

Trotsky, when he was appointed Foreign Commissar, arrived at his ministry to find a staff meeting in progress. Prince Urossov, the chairman, allowed him to address it, whereupon he announced that in the new era all members of public institutions must support the workers' and peasants' Revolution, and that all from himself down to the junior doorkeeper would receive equal pay. His elegantly attired audience smiled cynically; most of them, having been people of means, had accepted the honour of membership of the foreign service for no salary at all. Prince Urossov made a brief speech in reply, stressing the independence of the civil service, and the uncomfortable silence that followed was broken by a typist, who inquired whether the new minister's real name was not Trotsky but Bronstein. Amid general laughter Trotsky replied lamely that the Revolution had given him a new name, whereupon an official of the Political Department, who had hitherto been remarkable only for his shyness, declared that it was a bad thing to take a false name. Being at a loss what to say, Trotsky inquired 'What is your name?' 'My name is Chemersin,' the man replied proudly, 'and Chemersin it will remain.'[3] It was an empty gesture. Chemersin was a marked man from that moment, and soon acquired new papers under the name of Ivanov.

'I shall never forget those dreary rainy days of November', wrote Korostovetz. 'Equipped with goloshes and umbrellas, carefully peering about, and slinking from corner to corner, we went to attend the meetings of our Union of Civil Servants. These meetings were held first in one place, then

The storming of the Winter Palace, Petrograd, 1917

In the summer of 1917, the Provisional Government organised a women's shock
battalion which was to guard the Winter Palace. This photograph shows them taking
an oath in Moscow's Red Square, July 1917

Cadets guard members of the Provisional Government in the Winter Palace on the
eve of the October Revolution

in another, to escape the vigilance of the Bolsheviks. They would start with reports of the situation "at the front"; then followed patriotic speeches, and resolutions were unanimously passed to continue the strike up to the convocation of the Constituent Assembly – "the Master of the Russian Earth", as it was then called. These resolutions were heliographed by fearless men who worked at them night after night in their own rooms, and then distributed them among our members. One could never be certain that one was not going to be betrayed by some minor official whom the Bolsheviks had bribed with the promise of a high position. So, before setting out, everyone put a few sandwiches in his pocket to avoid starving in the cellars of the Smolny.'[4]

The Smolny Institute was now the seat of all power. In July Kerensky had persuaded the Soviet organizations that had established themselves in the Tauride Palace, the splendid meeting-place of the Imperial Duma, to make room for the coming Constituent Assembly. They commandeered this boarding school for the daughters of the nobility, the young ladies having long since fled; and it was from this incongruous setting that the Military Revolutionary Committee had directed the October Revolution. Now, with the assumption of all authority by the Congress of Soviets, its Executive Committee and the Council of People's Commissars, it had become the place from which Russia was governed.

In December the civil service strike petered out for lack of financial resources, the 'underground' Provisional Government was dispersed and the various Committees for Salvation around the country silently dissolved. The bourgeoisie, deprived of all their political institutions, began to look for deliverance outside themselves. Perhaps, they thought, the Council of People's Commissars would collapse from the sheer impossibility of governing; or the once-hated Germans would capture Petrograd and restore some sort of order.

But there was another hope, too, which was to prove the most deceptive of all and bring untold misery on Russia. General Kaledin, Ataman of the Don Cossacks, had made a speech at the Moscow State Conference in August that had later led Kerensky to suspect that he was involved in the

Kornilov Affair. An order was given for his arrest, but the Don Cossacks, who had set up an independent republic of their own, refused to hand him over.

Meanwhile Kornilov and his fellow-conspirators, including General Denikin, were in prison near Mogilev, awaiting trial for treason. They were the responsibility of General Dukhonin, the last of the Provisional Government's commanders-in-chief. The Bolsheviks confirmed his appointment, and instructed him to open armistice negotiations with the Germans. He ignored the order and was dismissed, his high office being granted to a junior officer known to Lenin, Ensign Krylenko. On 21 November, the day on which this young man arrived at Mogilev accompanied by a contingent of armed sailors, one of them shot Dukhonin dead. Also on that day (4 December, New Style) formal negotiations for an armistice began at Brest-Litovsk.

Krylenko did not find the Kornilov conspirators at Mogilev. Dukhonin had released them a few hours before his death, and they had taken the fateful decision to make their way south by various routes to join Kaledin at Novocherkassk. Alekseiev was already there, beginning to form his 'Volunteer Army' out of refugee officers and others who were escaping from Bolshevik-held territory.

This was a foretaste of civil war. It was also the beginning of intervention, for the Allies were now convinced that the only chance of keeping Russia in the war was to give military aid to centres of anti-Bolshevik resistance. Civil war and intervention spelled the final doom of the Russian propertied classes.

Yet in Petrograd and Moscow this was not yet realized. There was still the Cadet Party there, that once-proud organization that had taken over the government of Russia from the Tsar amid the plaudits of the world. Milyukov and other well-known leaders had fled, but in the city dumas of Petrograd and Moscow the Cadets had representations of 34 per cent and 17 per cent respectively. There was enough of the party machine left to organize public meetings in Petrograd as part of an election campaign for the Constituent Assembly.

Persecution began soon enough, however. On 9 November

all bourgeois newspapers were suppressed, and the Cadet offices in Moscow were forcibly closed. On 18 November the Cadet club in Petrograd was wrecked, and on 28 November the whole party were declared to be 'enemies of the people'.

At dawn that morning Countess Panina's apartment was raided, and she was arrested along with Shingarev, Koko-shkin and Prince Dolgorukov, as they were preparing to attend a preliminary meeting of the Constituent Assembly. Trotsky announced proudly:

'We have made a modest beginning. We have arrested the Cadet leaders and have given orders that the Cadets in the provinces should be carefully watched. At the time of the French Revolution more honest men than the Cadets were guillotined by the Jacobins for opposing the people. We have not executed anyone, and do not intend to do so, but there are moments when the fury of the people is hard to control. The Cadets had better take warning.'

Later Countess Panina was charged with sequestring 93,000 roubles from the Ministry of Education. Hers was the first case brought before the new Revolutionary Tribunal, which sat in the palace of the absent Grand Duke Nicholas, under P. I. Stutchka, the Commissar for Justice.

This was the Bolsheviks' first and only failure in the art of holding show trials. The intrepid Countess admitted that she had taken the money, but said she was holding it in trust for the legitimate government that would be established by the Constituent Assembly. She was popular at that time for the work she had done to further the education of the masses. Meetings in her support were held in the People's Palace, and protests were made by the Faculty Council of the university and by twenty-eight social and educational associations. At the trial a humble munitions worker named N. I. Ivanov spoke movingly on her behalf. The court felt able to do no more than send her to prison until the money was repaid. All classes joined in collecting the sum, and she was freed on 19 December.

The liberals now took new heart. The suppressed Cadet

newspaper *Rech* reappeared daily under new names, and more public meetings were organized. At these the phrase 'enemies of the people' was greeted with ironic laughter by bourgeois audiences. A regional party conference was held in Moscow on 17 December, at which plans were made for a new library and for 'an agitational course for party workers'.

But this gleam of light soon flickered out. Already the Bolsheviks were revealing their intention to interfere with, and ultimately destroy, the private lives of the rich.

The second Revolution itself had been effected with none of the incidental excesses of the first. There had been no murders or massacres of officers during those 'ten days that shook the world', few private cars had been requisitioned, and well-dressed people had moved about Petrograd without molestation.

It was not long, however, before these well-dressed people realized what had hit them. On 10 November Peter the Great's Table of Ranks was formally abolished. On 22 November every citizen with more than one fur coat was ordered to hand over the others to the army; this gave Red Guards and local party officials a pretext for searching the houses of the rich. On 11 December control of education was taken from the Church. On 14 December banking, at least in theory, became a State monopoly, workers' control of industry was established, and commercial secrecy was abolished. On 16 December all army ranks were officially suppressed, except for the purely operational one of 'commander'. After 17 December houses could no longer be bought and sold. On 18 December civil marriage and divorce were instituted. On 21 December the 'revolutionary courts' were given a code that almost made the legal profession otiose. On 24 December Putilov's vast factories were confiscated. On 29 December payment of interest and dividends was stopped. Private bank accounts were frozen, and depositors were permitted to draw only 125 roubles a week.

· Not all these decrees could be put into force at once, even in that part of Russia that the Bolsheviks claimed to govern. Until some new economic structure came into being, commercial activity continued; nevertheless, the old structure was now fatally undermined.

All appearances, however, did not suddenly change. The *Manchester Guardian* man Price noted in December that in Petrograd traffic was normal.

'The bourgeoisie could be distinguished by their better dresses and expensive furs. Cinemas were filled. The well-to-do went to the theatres and Chaliapin sang to crowded middle-class audiences every night. Newspaper boys sold Cadet and other bourgeois newspapers and journals, which were predicting the imminent fall of Smolny. It was often difficult to buy the official Soviet newspapers or the organs of the Bolsheviks and the Left S.R.s. The private banks stood behind the bourgeois editors and Smolny had not yet dared to put its hand on this holy of holies of capitalism. The capitalist State was working merrily on, in spite of all the thundering of Smolny.'[5]

Pasternak, in *Dr Zhivago*, described this social dichotomy, which recalled the political dichotomy of the era of Dual Government at the beginning of the year:

'The old life and the new ways did not yet interlock. They were not as yet at daggers drawn, as when the civil war broke out a year later, but neither did they have much connection with each other. They were like two parts of a puzzle set down side by side and which could not be made to fit.

'Everywhere there were new elections: for the running of housing, trade, industry and municipal services. Commissars were being appointed to each, men in black leather jerkins, with unlimited powers and an iron will, armed with means of intimidation and revolvers, who shaved little and slept less. They knew the shrinking bourgeois breed, the average holders of cheap government stocks, and they spoke to them without the slightest pity and with Mephistophelian smiles, as to petty thieves caught in the act. These were the people who reorganized everything in accordance with the plan, and company after company, enterprise after enterprise, became bolshevized.'[6]

In one sense the nationalizing of the banks was a failure, because the bank clerks went on strike, and the Red Guards who burst in on them were incapable of carrying on such an intricate business. In another sense, however, it was a mortal blow to the bourgeoisie. Their strength depended on their being able to manipulate an orderly system, and they were helpless in conditions of financial chaos.

A new race of small entrepreneurs had emerged beneath their feet – men who knew how to get government contracts for the supply of certain goods. These were not former men of substance, or even dismissed heads of old firms, who were incapable of manipulating the new situation. They were spivs who saw their brief opportunity, and took it.

Street disturbances began again. Petrograd in November was full of self-demobilized soldiers, undisciplined Red Guards, common criminals who had been released from gaol along with the political prisoners, and workers un-employed because of the scarcity of raw materials. The prohibition of the public sale of alcohol imposed by the Tsar at the beginning of the war had not been rescinded, and it now occurred to these idlers that there was a plentiful supply of wine and spirits in the cellars of the rich. Night after night these were broken into, and there were appalling scenes of mass drunkenness, leading sometimes to loss of life. The Bolshevik authorities did not approve of this lack of revolutionary discipline and did their best to restrain it, but it was not until they drafted into the city Lettish troops and Finnish and Estonian sailors that they were able to control the situation.

Similar scenes were enacted in the countryside, where vodka was still being produced on big estates, nominally for industrial purposes. Few of the distilleries were spared, and many landlords suffered at the hands of peasants who, when sober, had been peaceable.

Great possessions were already becoming an embarrassment, and rich Moscow merchants like Shchukin and Morozov started to present some of their art treasures to the State, in the hope of buying off the confiscations they foresaw would soon come. This was the foundation of the Pushkin Gallery, which to this day delights visitors with examples of western painting, particularly of French Impressionists. Nothing could have exemplified better the enormous wealth that had been concentrated in a few Russian hands or the cultivated taste that it had sometimes inspired – a taste not shared by the philistine imperial family.

But it was the wine that impressed the populace most. Crimean vintages were not of the highest quality, which meant that the Russian upper classes, like those of England, had developed a palate for the products of all the best wine-growing countries of Europe. Not being by nature abstemious they laid down enormous cellars. These, too, to avoid drunken orgies, were in many cases donated to the State 'for the hospitals'. If any reached that destination before being pilfered by Bolshevik officials, the patients, though otherwise ill-tended, were singularly fortunate in their medicine.

The Grand Duke Paul and Princess Paley fell neatly into a trap in the matter of their own magnificent cellar. A Bolshevik official arrived to say that it was about to be searched, and suggested that if they concealed their choicest vintages in various parts of the palace, leaving the more ordinary stocks to be discovered, he would for a consideration, not betray their secret. They eagerly embraced this ruse, but when the raid took place the man denounced them. They lost almost the lot – 10,000 bottles in all – and were forced to pay a crippling fine.

In such a nightmare world, in which nothing was stable, people found distraction where they could. Some of the bourgeoisie haunted the cafés of the revolutionary poets and artists, who, emerging from the frustrating period of the Provisional regime, now felt free to give rein to their most extreme fantasies.

It was the millionaire Filipov who financed the most celebrated bohemian establishment of all, the Poets' Café in Moscow's Nastasyinsky Alley.

'It was a most peculiar place', wrote Ilya Ehrenburg. 'The walls were covered with paintings that must have looked very strange to the public, and with sentences that were no less strange. "I like watching children die" – that line from Mayakovsky's early pre-revolutionary poem was to be seen on the wall to shock those who entered.

'The Poets' Cafe was not at all like the Rotunda. No one talked art there, there were no discussions; those present were divided into actors and spectators. The audience consisted of the remnants of the bourgeoisie – profiteers, writers, philistines in search of entertainment. Everyone could understand Mayakovsky's song about the bourgeois eating pineapples toward the end of his days. There were no pineapples in Nastasyinsky Alley, but a morsel of ordinary pork stuck in some people's throats. Those who visited the place were entertained by something else. For instance, David Burliuk would mount the platform, his face heavily powdered, lorgnette in hand, and recite "I like pregnant men" '.[7]

Mayakovsky, in mid-December, wrote to some friends: 'Moscow is like a ripe, swelling fruit, which Dodya, Kamensky and I are zealously picking. The main place where the picking goes on is the Poets' Cafe. We send the public to the devil. At midnight we divide the till. That's all.'[8]

The proletariat, too, were subjected to this kind of nonsense. Ehrenburg wrote:

'Every morning the inhabitants carefully studied the new decrees, still wet and crumpled, pasted on the walls: they wanted to know what was permitted and what was forbidden. One day I saw a gathering of people standing in front of a small sheet of paper entitled "Decree Number 1 on the Democratization of Art". Someone was reading it aloud: "From this day forth, with the abolition of Tsardom, the domicile of art in the closets and sheds of human genius – palaces, galleries, salons, libraries, theatres – is abrogated." An old woman shrieked: "All saints have mercy, now they are taking sheds away." The man in spectacles who was reading the "decree" aloud explained: "There is nothing here about sheds, but they will close libraries and, of course, theatres." The leaflet was the work of Futurists and was signed by Mayakovsky, Kamensky and Burliuk. The names meant nothing to the passers-by, but everybody knew the magic word "decree".

'This decree was certainly a puzzler. It ordained that "the free word of creative personality" should be written not only on walls, roofs, motorcars and trams but "on the clothes of all citizens"; as for pictures, they had to be "thrown, like coloured rainbows, across streets and squares, from house to house, delighting and ennobling the eye of the passer-by. From now on, let the citizen walking down the street enjoy at every moment the depths of thought of his great contemporaries, let him absorb the flowery gaudiness of this day's beautiful joy, let him listen to music – the melody, the roar, the buzz – of excellent composers everywhere." [9]

In an 'Open Letter to the Workers' published in the *Futurists' Journal*, Mayakovsky wrote:

'I observe with astonishment how renowned theatres resound with *Aidas* and *Traviatas*, with their Spaniards and counts; how in the poems to which you listen the same noblemen's hothouse-roses are flowering; how your eyes are opening wide in front of pictures showing the pomp of the past. Will you, perhaps, when the elements let loose by Revolution quieten down, go out on Sunday into the squares before your local soviet buildings, with watchchains on your waistcoats, and stolidly play croquet? You should know that for your necks, the necks of Goliaths of labour, there are no sizes in the bourgeois collar box that fit. Only the outburst of the Spirit of Revolution will rid us of the rags of old art. Snatch greedily the big healthy chunks of young brutal art which we give you. No one can know what immense suns will light our future lives. It may be that artists will turn the grey dust of cities into multicoloured rainbows, that the never-ending thunderous music of volcanoes turned into flutes will resound from mountain ranges; that ocean waves will be forced to play on the nets of chords stretching from Europe to America. One thing is clear to us – we have opened the first page of the latest chapter in the history of art.' [10]

Side by side with all this, a more traditional form of entertainment was still available to the remaining rich. Contant's restaurant was popular because it had managed to keep its wine cellar safe by installing a score of hefty chaps provided with rifles, machine guns and grenades whom it paid, fed, and supplied with drink in abundance.

On 2 November Count Lucien de Robien entertained the French industrialist Armand de Saint-Sauveur there.

'Dinner was excellent, and a lot of people were there. Gulenko played the *Nord Express* with more gusto than ever, but I must admit I was rather irritated by this gang of twenty strapping fellows striving to amuse a few idlers, when people were killing each other perhaps a few versts away. But then that is Russia in a nutshell, with its morbid charm, its contrasts and its incoherence.'[11]

One night some sailors came into Contant's brandishing revolvers and forced the diners to empty their pockets, to satisfy themselves that these bourgeois were unarmed. They stole nothing.

On another occasion a solitary comrade came in and sat down at one of the tables. From there he beckoned to the numerous officers in the room who, as they were not in the street, had kept on their epaulettes.

'He called them over to him,' wrote Robien, '... psst ... psst ... and then pointed to the door. Those concerned quickly understood, obeyed and went out; then returned, having deposited their epaulettes and badges of rank in the vestibule. They went on with their dinner unabashed, while listening to Gulenko playing dashing tunes on the piano.'[12]

The gaiety was forced, because there was now no personal security for any member of the upper classes who had escaped molestation at the time of the two revolutions. Early in November the elderly Grand Duke Paul was arrested as a security risk, though in fact he was living a completely idle life in his sumptuous palace at Tsarskoye Selo. He was taken to Smolny, where he had no complaints about his guards, some of whom addressed him as 'Comrade Highness'. They found an armchair for him; one of them begged him to read *Pravda* for them and explain it; and they obtained his permission to smoke while listening. He was released shortly afterwards on the grounds of ill-health.

Princess Paley, his morganatic wife, was much exercised at this time over the servant problem. Before the war she had commanded 64 domestics; these were reduced to 48 after the first revolution; and now, poor woman, she had only 22.

Humbler gentlewomen were less fortunate. On 23 December a deputation of about twenty Russian officers' wives came to the French Embassy to ask for help.

'It was pathetic', said Robien, 'to see these unfortunate women, who had been used to a certain comfort, still wearing fur coats and decent clothes, but reduced to begging, as most of them had no knowledge of any profession. Their husbands live the life of convicts in the barracks. They only get a private's pay of about 15 roubles, and the soldiers prevent them from working outside and earning more money.'[13]

One of these ladies told Robien that her husband, a Guards officer, had managed to escape and had spent the night unloading sacks of coal at the railway station, but the comrades found out and confiscated the few roubles he had earned with such difficulty.

Just before Christmas, near Cinizelli Circus, Robien saw 'an old general and a priest – the old Russia itself – clearing the streets of snow. A gang of soldiers, in the prime of life, stood and mocked them.'[14]

University professors, too, were all now in straitened circumstances, and were obliged to undertake manual work to live.

In the countryside, for the rich, life was a strange mixture of peace and horror, as Galina von Meck discovered. She was a grandniece of Tchaikovsky's patroness and daughter of Nicholas von Meck, president of the largest privately-owned railway company in Russia, and a friend of the Grand Duchess Elizabeth. She had made an unhappy marriage with an English gentleman farmer, who had become an estate manager near Batum. In October he received his call-up papers from Britain, and caught a train from Petrograd on the day after the fall of the Provisional Government. His wife was given the job of manager of Yerush, a 20,000-acre forest in Tambov Province belonging to her father's railway company. After seeing her husband off, she arrived back in Moscow in the middle of the fighting there. There was a panic exodus from the city, but her father, for the last time, was able to arrange for her to complete her journey in state, travelling in his private coach.

'We had our illusions during those early days', she wrote. 'There were horrors, but there was also a belief in the future that kept my father's spirits up. He was sure that the Revolution was a transient phase, a path leading to a new life. He always insisted that every Russian should help no matter what fate had in store for him. To run away at such a time was unpardonable.'[15]

The first wave of destruction broke out suddenly. Surrounding estates were pillaged or set on fire. Some owners fled, others were thrown out.

On the estate of Prince Engalychev, a member of the railway board, the mob broke into the well-stocked wine cellar. They staggered on, drunk, to the church. Men and women put on the priestly vestments and took the chalice from the altar. A man and his wife used the holy shroud to cover a sledge loaded with potatoes.

The destruction continued for about ten days. Every night the sky around Yermish was red with the glow of fires.

Even the Bolshevik authorities were against this indiscriminate violence in advance of a final settlement of the land question, and troops were sent to stop it. Landowners began to drift back to their homes. The couple who had used the holy shroud could not sleep, imagining they heard a voice wailing outside their house all through the hours of darkness. Other peasants who had taken part in the looting also heard mysterious noises. The villagers assembled to listen to Galina, the two parish priests and the schoolmaster. They returned everything to the church, as bells pealed from the church tower, and a short service of reparation was held.

The young Princess Shakhovskoi, whom we last heard of leaving her boarding school for young ladies in Petrograd on the morrow of the February Revolution, spent a more peaceful winter on her parents' estate in the Tula Province.

At Matovo, the Princess wrote, 'my father was free of cares. We returned to him with relief. The house in Empire style, a little disfigured by the buildings added periodically as the family increased, the garden in full bloom, the old servants, the reassuring friendliness of peasants who had known us for generations and were grateful for the help my family had given them during past epidemics and famines – this seemed a sure haven. We proceeded, in a mood of good neighbourliness, to apportion the land; we turned out, without pleasure but philosophically enough, to watch the felling of the woods which had once belonged to us. My father lost his title of Prince to become the "comrade estate-holder" without any corresponding change in our relationship with the peasants. My parents remained their advisers. Without tears or gnashing of teeth, the Commune of Matovo was born.

'Elsewhere, the revolutionary hurricane was carrying all before it. Matovo became an autarchy in which every trade was represented: tailor, miller, shoemaker, tanner, etc. Large enough stocks of wheat, fats, and smoked and salted meat had been laid in to stave off the approaching threat of famine. There were sufficient arms and ammunition – including grenades brought back from the front – to withstand a siege. Each of us had his or her responsibilities, willingly accepted. Mine were those of poulterer. The boys mowed the hay as if they had never done anything else in their lives. We learned to milk the cows, to thresh the corn, to mill the flour. And, between labours, we had our usual pleasures; evenings around the piano, hunting, reading, editing a newspaper, the *Matovo Messenger*, which bore on its title page the "counter-revolutionary" arms of the Shakhovskois.'[16]

Since nothing could be bought any more, the family discovered in the attics hidden treasures of their grandfathers' times – sumptuous overcoats for coachmen of best quality green cloth and old curtains of gorgeous velvet from which ladies' gowns could be made.

A traditional Christmas was spent, with sleigh rides to the church of a neighbouring and very friendly village. On New Year's Day the young folk and children, accompanied by the servants, all in fancy dress, went to Matovo village, where everybody greeted the masqueraders with delight.

This was the last of the old Russian Christmases. Princess

Paley managed a modest little tree, contrasting strangely with the superb one of the previous year. The presents were also modest, for the Grand Duke Paul's income was greatly reduced. No one came, as there were hardly any trains and few private cars or carriages.

Four days later it was the twenty-first birthday of the Princess's son, Vladimir, by her previous marriage. They relit the candles on the tree, and his two little half-sisters, Irene and Nathalie, acted a play in verse that he had written called *The Delft Plate*.

Then came New Year's Day. It was difficult to believe that twelve months before the Diplomatic Corps had driven out to Tsarskoye Selo to present their compliments to the Tsar at a smooth and resplendent Court ceremony. This time there was more serious business afoot. Twenty Allied and neutral heads of mission, representing, apart from the Central Powers, all the civilized States of Europe, America and Asia, formed a long procession of carriages, with gold-braided *chasseurs* on the front seats, to go to Smolny to make a protest to Lenin. This concerned the unprecedented arrest of the Rumanian Minister and his staff, as a reprisal for steps taken by the Rumanian Government to curb excesses committed by Russian troops on Rumanian soil.

The Allied representatives were in a difficult position. They had not recognized the new regime, but still claimed diplomatic privileges, and were trying to dissuade Lenin and Trotsky from making a separate peace with Germany.

On this occasion the Rumanian Minister was released, but life was no longer easy for these cosmopolitans who a year before had been moving so pleasantly in high Petrograd society. There were no gay parties for this New Year, all the restaurants were closed, and not a single servant was on duty in the smart Hotel de l'Europe.

Meanwhile everyone was waiting for the meeting, scheduled at last for early January, of the Constituent Assembly. This was the apocalyptic event which all Russia, except for a hard core of reactionaries, had been dreaming about for half a century and more. Nihilists, socialists, liberals, enlightened monarchists – all had acknowledged this ideal parliament, to be elected by direct, secret and universal suffrage, as the future 'Master of the Russian Earth'. No Petrograd Soviet, no All-Russian Congress of Soviets, no Council of People's Commissars, could in theory challenge its sovereignty.

Now at length, during November, it had been elected, by 42 million citizens; and the proportion of votes was not at all to Lenin's liking: moderate socialists 58 per cent, Bolsheviks and their allies 29 per cent, Cadets and other bourgeois parties, 13 per cent.

This was the country's answer to the October Revolution. 71 per cent of the electorate rejected it, and the Social-Revolutionaries, the party that stood for the gradual building of socialism within a capitalist framework, had been returned with an absolute majority.

The liberals were overjoyed. This was parliamentary democracy, to which they were committed. They were a minority, but in a parliamentary democracy minorities have rights. They began to foresee a constitution that would facilitate, not another coalition, but a socialist government which, with their help, would begin to restore the economic and social order.

On 16 November the ghost of the former Provisional Government issued a 'decree' summoning the Constituent Assembly to meet immediately. It was signed by S. Prokopovich as 'acting Prime Minister', and P. Maliantovich, as 'Minister of Justice'. Ten days later the former Cadet ministers in prison, led by Konovalov, managed to smuggle out an 'act of State', formally handing over power to the Assembly. Naturally, the new government took no notice, and next day proceeded to do a little more tidying up by abolishing the Senate.

This was the last of the Cadets' dreams, except for those built on fantasies fed later by the civil war and the intervention. It was the last of the Right Social-Revolutionaries' dreams too. When the Constituent Assembly finally met on 5 January 1918 it was under the guns of Lettish guards. In spite of this, under the chairmanship of the S.R. leader Chernov, a motion that it should recognize the Congress of Soviets as the government of Russia was defeated by 237 votes to 136. The Bolsheviks then withdrew, and the Assembly rushed through a series of resolutions that would have rebuilt Russia on moderate socialist lines. But in the early hours of the morning a soldier put his hand on the president's arm and told him that the guards were tired and that the meeting must disperse. All the members of the Master of the Russian Earth were led away in groups, to be, as Trotsky put it, 'thrown on the rubbish-heap of history'.

Thus, on 6 January 1918, Russian democracy, that had been so long gestating, was still-born.

11

Bolshevism

And now, on the hapless bourgeoisie, the blows fell thick and fast. 'We are living in a madhouse', wrote Robien, towards the end of January, in the comparative security of the French Embassy in Petrograd.

Not all the new laws could be enforced at once, but they indicated the shape of things to come. A decree was issued confiscating private houses, and confining their former owners to a few rooms in them. Special luxury taxes were levied on servants, on bathrooms, even on pianos. All non-workers under fifty were obliged to join the Personal Labour Corps. Under this, Princess Obolensky was ordered to clear the snow off the Fontanka Quay.

Another decree laid down that all jewellery and gold objects weighing more than 70 grammes, as well as all foreign currency, must be surrendered to the State. To this end, owners were commanded to attend at the banks and to open their safe-deposits. According to one such victim, 'Most of the holders appeared composedly with their keys and looked on with resignation at the confiscation of their property. Some did not utter a word; some excitedly tried to prove to the officials that this or that item was not subject to confiscation; others, amid tears, attempted to convince them that the valuables in the safe deposit boxes constituted all their property, without which they must starve. The officials were in a difficult position. They could not show any clemency and had to adhere strictly to their instructions.'[1] Some rich people recovered their boxes in advance by heavily bribing the bank clerks, who were shot if the deal was discovered.

During March and April there was a brief pause on the economic front. The almost total collapse of industry caused Lenin to call for a 'breathing-spell' in the matter of nationalization. Meshchersky, a Moscow businessman, was allowed to try to form a great metallurgical trust under State ownership in which former proprietors would participate in the management and profits. The Stakhaev Company proposed a similar arrangement in the Urals, and another group of financiers put forward a scheme for the establishment of international trading companies to engage in barter with France, the United States and Japan. There was even a proposal to invite American capital to participate in the exploitation of fishing and mining in Siberia. The Council of Representatives of Trade and Industry still existed, and was emboldened to protest against the favoured treatment given to German imports after Brest-Litovsk, and against the difficulties of obtaining credits from the nationalized banks.

But the intensification of the civil war soon caused all projects of co-operation between the State and private industry to be abandoned. The breathing-spell came to an end, and Soviet Russia entered the phase of War Communism.

Gradually full economic totalitarianism was established. The general plan of nationalization was published in June. By November all commercial capital had been expropriated, and domestic trade and small-scale industry nationalized. In December even the people's co-operatives were integrated in the State machine. Strikes were declared treason, the trade unions lost their new power, and 'food armies' were formed to requisition grain from the peasants.

The old country life of the squires had now vanished completely. On 9 February Gorky's newspaper reported that the summer palace of the former governor of Riazan had been destroyed, with the destruction of pictures, art objects and furniture worth a million roubles. 'The peasant women grabbed the Sèvres vases, and now use them for sour cream.'

From Kharkov there was news that the Kropivnitsky collection of rare books, pictures, manuscripts and notes was no more. In Simbirsk the home of the historian Karamzin was destroyed, along with the villa of Prince Kurakin, with its priceless collection of eighteenth-century engravings. In the Penza province the fury of the mob was so great that villas and palaces were set on fire with everything in them.

On 22 March the same newspaper stated that many landowners of Simbirsk had had everything taken from them. 'They have tried to become members of the peasants' organizations so as to remain in the village and receive at least something to keep them from starving. The peasants, however, take a hostile attitude towards these "bloodsuckers". They either will not admit them at all, or else demand an impossible entrance fee. In a few cases the "bloodsuckers" have paid their fee and been admitted, but have later been expelled, losing, of course, their money.'

After the dispersal of the Constituent Assembly, political resistance was no longer possible in 'Sovdepia', the central territory controlled by the Bolsheviks. All former Cadet ministers who had not escaped southwards or abroad were in prison. Two of the most prominent, Alexander Shingarev and Feodor Kokoskin, author of the electoral law, were killed by Red sailors while under guard in hospital, and no serious attempt was made to apprehend and punish the murderers.

The Central Committee of the Cadet Party did meet for a time in various private Moscow apartments, with a sentry posted outside to warn them against possible arrest. Much soul-searching took place at these gatherings. Was it still possible to maintain the principles of liberalism, or did the only hope lie in supporting a military dictatorship such as that which Generals Alexeiev and Kornilov seemed to be planning in the Caucasus? The acting chairman, P. I. Novgorodtsev, regretfully favoured the latter course, to be pursued by 'individual action', and his view prevailed. Liberalism, as an organized force in central Russian politics, expired, and its standard-bearer, the Cadet Party, died with it.

Individual action meant the end of the loyalty to the Allies that had previously been the mark of the party. Milyukov, who had been so vehement in accusing the Autocracy of being secretly pro-German, transferred his allegiance, in the safety of the Ukraine, in the hope that it would be the Kaiser's troops who would set up a constitutional monarchy under some acceptable Romanov. Other Cadets put their faith in the Allies.

The Bolsheviks, for their part, were facing the danger of a German occupation of Petrograd, and steeling themselves to sign, instead, the Brest-Litovsk treaty whereby Russia was to lose a third of her population, a quarter of her territory and more than half her industry. As for the remnants of the bourgeoisie in the capital, they would have preferred a German occupation to peace. Robien met people on the Nevsky Prospect 'radiant with joy' at the thought of this national disaster. 'I understand the feelings of our Russian friends', he wrote; 'they have suffered too much for me not to forgive them. But they are really a little lacking in shame, and ought to show their pleasure in a less demonstrative way.'[2]

The Revolution, as Sir Paul Vinogradov wrote, had 'meant the overthrow of all accepted creeds, morals and habits of the people, a confusion of their entire nature, in which, for a time, nothing could be relied upon – neither duty, nor humanity, nor affection'.[3]

At this stage only the Church put up any kind of institutional opposition to the Bolsheviks, and that was on a very narrow front. The new government had deprived it of its vast lands and of its various secular privileges, including the supervision of education, but, to emphasize its separation from the State, had reversed Peter the Great's policy of putting the Patriarchate into commission under a lay minister and had allowed it to appoint its own spiritual head. Tikhon, the first patriarch for two centuries, proved to be a stout defender of the purely sacral aspects of Orthodoxy. When the Bolsheviks, seeking better accommodation than Smolny, occupied that holy of holies the Alexander Nevsky monastery in Petrograd, killing a monk in the process, he boldly pronounced an anathema against them.

He also ordered an expiatory procession, which the Bolsheviks at first banned but at the last moment thought it more prudent to authorize. Robien went to watch it.

'There was an enormous crowd, in which a lot of men were walking about bare-headed, carrying ikons and singing hymns. As I watched I had a vision of the old Russia of the past. The solemn chanting of the hymns, sung in parts by the choirs, was a rest from the revolutionary tunes to which we had become accustomed. Banners with a mellow patina and gleams of tarnished gold floated above the heads of the crowd and were a change from the lurid red standards whose startling colour has for the last year proclaimed itself stridently above the dark mass of the demonstrators and the whiteness of the snow. All this created an impression of strength, the strength of ancient, ignorant Russia, superstitious and formidable. There were no incidents, and as the procession went past Red Guards and soldiers observed a respectful silence and uncovered their heads.'[4]

On the following Sunday the anathema was proclaimed in all churches in Russia, and the Bolsheviks restored the monastery to the monks.

After this success, the Church became somewhat more political. Patriarch Tikhon condemned the treaty of Brest-Litovsk as surrendering millions of Orthodox believers to the rule of Lutherans and Roman Catholics. At a demonstration in the Red Square in Moscow he called on the faithful to 'go to their Golgotha', and leaflets were distributed condemning the Bolsheviks as 'sons of the Antichrist'. In October 1918, after the Patriarch had accused the Government of responsibility for almost every current evil, he was put under house arrest, but he was released the following Easter.

This was not yet the time of militant State atheism, for Lenin was afraid of withdrawal symptoms if the people were deprived too suddenly of their 'opium'. The Government did its best to dissuade Red Guards from invading churches at service-time defiantly smoking cigarettes. Parish churches, though now without their glebes, were entrusted to the care of their congregations. Seminaries continued to function, and religious instruction for children was permitted in private houses. A few political priests were executed during the civil war, but not specifically because they were priests.

Monasteries and nunneries, however, as corporate land-owners, got short shrift. Though a few places of pilgrimage were spared, like the Alexander Nevsky abbey itself, most conventional establishments were seized and turned into hospitals and schools. The investigating commissions, in the manner of Thomas Cromwell, took a delight in exposing frauds concerning the relics of saints.

In March, with the German armies still advancing, Lenin blandly decided to do what he had previously condemned Kerensky for planning, and transfer the seat of government to Moscow. Remote Petrograd had fulfilled its revolutionary role, and the sensible thing now was to shake loose from this artificial capital of the Tsars and rule what remained of Russia from a firmer geographical base.

The Diplomatic Corps did not follow the Government. The Allied embassies sent military missions there, or to the H.Q. at Mogilev, but themselves moved to the little railway town of Vologda, which was considered a convenient place from which to escape if necessary, either by way of Arch-angel or across Siberia. There they endured a somewhat farcical existence in railway carriages and small bug-infested hotels, until the civil war and the approaching Allied interventions caused them to scatter.

Moscow did not at that time show the scars of revolution as much as Petrograd. Once the Tsar and his Court had fallen, his synthetic capital had taken on a completely new aspect, but the ancient capital and modern mercantile centre had a life of its own. It was an easier place to pro-vision, and remote from the front; and, because of the familiarity of its citizens with the ways of buying and selling, there was still a certain amount of money about, though in new hands. Many aristocrats and merchants were already starving, and a group of former officials of the Foreign Ministry had set up a shop there to sell, at fantastic prices, the silver, jewellery and porcelain of these *ci-devant*. The *nouveaux-riches* attained a certain elegance when they attended cabarets like the Chauve-Souris. Alongside the town's famous theatres, still flourishing, there were lively music-halls.

Moreover, in the shadow of the Kremlin, the external aspect of Russian religiosity did not vanish immediately. Robien noted during a visit in June: 'Here it really is Holy Russia. Everyone stops to cross himself by the Saviour's Gate, even though it is closed, and at the Chapel of the Virgin of Iberia queues of kneeling worshippers overflow into the street. One continually meets venerable landaus drawn by four horses abreast taking an ikon to heal some invalid or ward off some calamity.'[5]

Until the top Bolshevik politicians from Petrograd had time to transform the city, a few splendid houses continued to be occupied by their original owners. Robien stayed at the Kharitonenko Palace, where Princess Gorchakov was allowed to offer hospitality to the American and Italian missions.

'It is vast and sumptuous. The bathroom seems as large as a drawing-room and as high as a cathedral with its marble bath, its mirrors up to the ceiling, its porcelain-tiled floor covered in soft thick carpet, its dressing table with a pretty Dresden looking-glass, and its restful sofas.

'The palace occupies the most beautiful site in Moscow, opposite the Kremlin, which rises up on the other side of the river. The sumptuous interior is full of antique furniture, marbles and tapestries, and valuable paintings by Poussin, Corot, Troyon, Ziem and Diaz. When one realizes that on two occasions gangs of anarchists camped inside the house, forcing the owners to take refuge in a hotel, one must give them credit for the fact that nothing was damaged.'[6]

But a different form of artistry was to be seen in the streets. On the second revolutionary May Day Moscow was decorated with futurist and supremacist canvases. The day happened to fall in Holy Week, and the valiant Patriarch Tikhon tried in vain to ban all civil processions. Thus the old religion and the new came into conflict.

'By the Chapel of the Iberian Virgin there was a throng of praying people. Next to them lorries draped with abstract paintings were passing; actors on lorries were performing various scenes, such as "The Heroic Deed of Ivan Khulturin" or "The Paris Commune". An old woman, looking at a cubist painting with a huge fish eye, was lamenting: "They want us to worship Satan." '7

Two of the Kremlin ikons had been draped with red cloth. Whether by human agency or by the wind, this was torn from top to bottom, and there were many who attributed this to a miracle.

In Petrograd the Bolsheviks forbade the Holy Week children's marches, but they had to put up with the great procession on Easter Sunday. An enormous crowd walked along the Nevsky Prospect, in the wake of about a hundred priests in vestments.

In August and September 1918, Price of the *Manchester Guardian* maintained contacts with certain Moscow middle-class and aristocratic circles. He was living in the house of Count Sergei Tolstoy, the eldest son of the great Leo, in Levshinsky Street. The house had become a quiet meeting-place for forlorn aristocrats and Cadet politicians.

'The Count had developed some of his father's Christian-anarchist tendencies, condemned the old regime in Russia, and hankered after Henry George and the single tax. But ever and anon he remembered that he had once been a proud landlord, with whole villages that he could claim as his own, and his spirit rebelled against the "Red tyrants" who were destroying his "liberty".'8

Visitors came mostly after dark with their cloaks over their faces. They slept sometimes on the sofa in the drawing-room and disappeared before the sun rose. They were expecting midnight searches in their own dwellings by the Cheka, the new Bolshevik secret police. Among them were Prince Trubetskoy, ecclesiastical historian and Cadet politician, Prince Volkonsky, and various relatives of the Count's wife and sister.

'Some would be pro-Ally and some pro-German, but generally it was an unimportant matter to them which side won the war in Western Europe. For them there was only one question: how to reconcile Britain with Germany and secure the support of both for the overthrow of the Soviets. Germans, Allies, Japanese, Chinese, Indians – all were welcome in Russia if they would only re-establish these aristocrats in their ancestral privileges.'9

By this time 'Sovdepia' was fighting for its life. The treaty of Brest-Livotsk, ratified by the Fourth Congress of Soviets in March, had meant yielding up Estonia, Latvia, Lithuania and Russian Poland to Germany and Austria, recognizing the independence of the Ukraine, Georgia and Finland, and conceding large southern areas to Turkey. The Empire of All the Russias was almost reduced to the territory of the Grand Duchy of Muscovy.

The collapse of the Germans in November changed the situation, but did not relieve it. Tsarist generals had raised a White army on the Don and the Czechoslovak Legion was astride the Trans-Siberian railway. The British landed at Murmansk and Archangel and a five-nation Allied force at Vladivostok. Anti-Bolshevik regimes were set up in Siberia, Archangel, the Ukraine and Turkestan. Wherever the Whites were in control the old order was being re-established, often with great cruelty.

The aristocratic Prince A. Lobanov-Rostovsky, fighting with the White forces in the Crimea, decided that they were singularly ill-fitted to be the standard-bearers of the propertied classes.

'The bulk of the Volunteer Army was composed of former army officers, students and small clerks. These were all people of little means, drawing small salaries and certainly having only an academic interest in capitalism. Moreover they were all young. The man over fifty who might have accumulated a fortune had become such a conspicuous rarity that one stopped in the street to look at him. He either had been killed off by the hardships or was so crushed by events that he had become entirely inconspicuous.

'There seemed to be only one reality that bound the Whites together – an emotional hatred of the Reds. The Reds were responsible for all the woes that had befallen Russia, and that was sufficient – such was the dominating argument. The result was that the war was conducted with a ferocity rarely achieved in history. Each side saw in the opposing party not an enemy who had the right to stand up for his views but a traitor to a sacred cause. For the Reds, the Whites had betrayed the Revolution, and for the Whites the Reds had betrayed Russia. . . . One thing appeared certain: the White movement was not the promise of a new day, which it might have become if any constructive programme had been put forward, say along lines that later became fascism in Western Europe, or some other new creed alternative to communism which might have rallied the masses; instead it was the mere afterglow of a dead era.'[10]

The enmity between Generals Denikin and Wrangel became an open secret. It caused Lobanov to wonder whether, if the Whites won, Russia would become another China, with provincial war-lords fighting bitterly among themselves.

So this was civil war, in which whole classes could be regarded as traitors; and one Bolshevik method of waging civil war was to unleash terror against whole classes. It was back in December 1917, before the contemptuous dispersal of the Constituent Assembly, that the Bolsheviks had founded their own secret police, the Cheka. This dread name is composed of the initials of two Russian words which simply mean 'Extraordinary Commission'. The title is significant. The Cheka was indeed endowed with an extraordinary function, above and outside the law.

The Tsar's secret police, the Okhrana, had been an auxiliary organ of State power. Its purpose had been to keep watch on revolutionaries, extract information from them, sometimes by torture, and bring them to what then passed for justice. It had been charged with protecting an existing regime, and its only positive political action had been the organization of anti-Jewish pogroms as a relatively safe outlet for popular violence.

The function of the Cheka was quite different. This body was an offensive arm of the Bolshevik revolution, and it was given a free hand to destroy whatever stood in its way. Lenin, who before coming to power had dismissed simple terror as an infantile and ineffectual way of changing the basis of society, now saw it as a short cut towards moulding society into the pattern he desired. Nor was he above recruiting for this purpose a number of police agents who had formerly worked happily for the Tsar. As his grip on the country increased, so did the extra-legal role of the Extraordinary Commission.

The spread of this terror began at a time when the ordinary business of living was becoming daily more irksome. To the privations caused by the war and the economic breakdown were now added the intrusion by an impromptu and uneducated bureaucracy into every aspect of life, so that privacy and independence were impossible. Living in corners of their former homes, and sharing their declining amenities with rough and hostile strangers, the middle classes were trapped in a situation from which there was no escape. They became like inmates of a concentration camp, intent only on survival.

Alexander Solzhenitsyn, in *The Gulag Archipelago*, having quoted Lenin's proclaimed intention in January 1918 to 'purge the Russian land of all kinds of harmful insects', writes: 'It is not possible for us at this time fully to investigate exactly who fell within the broad definition of *insects*; the population of Russia was too heterogeneous and encompassed small special groups, entirely superfluous and, today, forgotten'.[11] But he numbers among these 'insects' former zemstvo members, people in the co-operative movement, home-owners, high school teachers, church parish councils and choirs, priests, monks and nuns, Tolstoyan pacifists and officials of the trade unions that had lost their brief moment of effective existence. These groups, he writes, represented 'an enormous number of people – several years' work of purge activity. In addition, how many kinds of cursed intellectuals there were – restless students and a variety of eccentrics, truth-seekers and holy fools, of whom even Peter the Great had tried in vain to purge Russia and who are always a hindrance to a well-ordered, strict regime'. For such people Lenin prescribed imprisonment, the duty of cleaning latrines or forced labour of the hardest kind.

To escape this fate, writes Solzhenitsyn, a few wives and daughters of the nobility and the officer-class offered their services to the Cheka as informers. They were useful because 'former' people trusted them. Among such he names the last Princess Vyazemskaya and Konkordiya Nikolayevna Iosse. The latter's officer husband had been shot in her sight, but she managed to beg her way out of exile to set up a salon near the Lubianka prison in Moscow for the benefit of Cheka officials, and was not rearrested until 1937.

Murder as a political weapon was first employed against the Tsar himself and his family. The Czechs were advancing on Ekaterinburg, their new place of detention in Siberia, and the local soviet dared not let the imperial family fall into enemy hands. On 3 July 1918 they and their four remaining faithful attendants were butchered in the cellar of the house where they were imprisoned.

All members of the Romanov family on whom the Bolsheviks could lay their hands met the same fate. Next day the Grand Duchess Elizabeth, who was the Empress's sister, the Grand Duke Serge Mikhailovich, three sons of the Grand Duke Constantine and Vladimir, son of the Grand Duke Paul, were thrown alive into an abandoned mineshaft outside the neighbouring town of Alapayesk. In the following January four more grand dukes were executed, including Paul, the Tsar's uncle, and Nicholas Mikhailovich, the liberal historian who had so much enjoyed himself, in pre-revolutionary days, jeering at the head of the family in the comfort of the English Club. When Gorky pleaded with Lenin for the life of this exceptional grand duke, Lenin replied: 'The revolution has no need of historians.'

The news of the imperial murders, which electrified the outside world, was received in Russia with comparative indifference. The revolution had rolled on so far since the abdication that the Tsar was almost a forgotten figure. Lenin interrupted a meeting of the Presidium of the Central Executive Council to allow the news to be announced, after which normal business was immediately resumed. Only the Allied representatives, now cowering at Vologda, assumed such mourning clothes as they still possessed. Ekaterinburg itself was captured by the Czechs eight days after the terrible event, and the pre-revolutionary style of life was quickly resumed there, with officers and their ladies strolling in the public gardens to the music of a military band. But in Moscow the Orthodox Patriarch sang a solemn requiem for the Church's former Protector.

Perhaps the remaining bourgeoisie in Bolshevik-held territory hoped that the sacrifice of a number of symbolic victims out of the past would appease the new masters of the land. They were soon disillusioned. The murder of the Romanovs was not a symbolic act, but a necessity of civil war. The Tsar and his relations were not the only potential nuclei of counter-revolution. All the former possessing classes shared this distinction, and, if they could not all be murdered, they could all be terrorized.

In September Lenin came to the conclusion that selective killings and the taking of hostages would damp the ardour of the White forces. The Left S.R. paper *Krasnaya Gazeta* attempted in vain to dissuade him.

'The bourgeoisie', it wrote on 5 September, 'have been taught a cruel lesson. Let our enemies leave us in peace to build a new life. If they do so, we shall ignore their simmering hatred and stop hunting them out. The Red Terror is over until the White Terror begins again. The destiny of the bourgeoisie is in its own hands.'

This was not Lenin's idea. More than 500 hostages had been taken in Petrograd – noblemen, officers of all ranks, right-wing journalists, industrialists, merchants – and it was proposed to shoot ten of them for every Communist who fell victim to the White Terror. In Moscow sixty hostages, including three former Tsarist ministers, were actually shot.

Typical September reports reaching Cheka headquarters were: from Penza, 'the murder of the worker Yegorov has been avenged by 152 lives'; from Kstroma, 'the big bourgeoisie are in our hands, and we are keeping them busy cleaning the barracks'; from Nizhny-Novgorod, 'forty-one priests, officers, police and capitalists killed'.

As M. Y. Latsis, one of the organizers of the Cheka wrote: 'The Extraordinary Commission is neither an investigating commission nor a tribunal. It is an organ of struggle, acting on the home front of the civil war. It does not judge the enemy; it strikes him.'

This ferocity was systematized, as the Cheka established its grip on the provinces. There was no point in using the terror weapon indiscriminately when it could be applied to specific political ends. The selected victims simply disappeared. The uncertainty left in the minds of their relatives and friends was a more powerful psychological weapon than the public announcement of their execution would have been. For this reason the Cheka conducted its investigations in secret, without allowing the right of defence. Executions were usually carried out in cellars, by revolver.

Eventually a census was taken of the whole bourgeois population, regardless of their supposed potential as counter-revolutionaries. From them the hostages were drawn.

In the first half of 1918 the Cheka executed twenty-two people; in the second half of the year, 6,000, and in 1919, 10,000. This was according to the official records, but W. H. Chamberlin estimated that by the end of 1920 no less than 50,000 people had been killed.

Compared with the mass murders of the Stalin era, when the Revolution began to devour its own children, these figures were not great. Nevertheless they had the effect of recruiting pre-revolutionary skills for the young Soviet state. Technicians and administrators of all kinds, who might have been considered privileged in the past, hastened to offer their services to the new authorities, in the hope of saving their lives.

Officers of the old Tsarist army had no choice. They were all ordered to report to the authorities of Trotsky's new Red Army. Five hundred of them were shot out of hand; the rest, numbering some 20,000, were recruited to fight against their former comrades.

In 1919 the Academy of Sciences recorded the deaths of fifty of its members 'from lack of nourishment or physical over-exertion'. The latter explanation referred to the manual labour that members of the educated classes were obliged to perform.

Only a few artists and thinkers who had been prominent under the old regime found an acceptable niche under the new. Gorky, of course, was a figure whom even Lenin could not ignore; Chaliapin went on singing old songs to new audiences; and Alexandre Benois continued for a time as artistic director to preside over the imperial theatres, now nationalised. 'The aesthetic trio', Zinaida Hippius called them, with envious contempt.

Two composers of the first rank, Stravinsky and Prokofiev, survived the Revolution, and were only later to learn that even music, to a Marxist, had a social content. Glazunov, who had been made director of the Petrograd Conservatoire, was less fortunate. When H. G. Wells visited him in his attic he begged, not for food, though he was starving, but for paper on which to write his compositions.

Valery Bryasov, leader of the Moscow symbolist poets, was given some educational work to do; A. F. Koni, who had been a member of the Imperial Senate, read historical lectures at the age of seventy-five to the Red Army; Alexander Blok continued to write until his death in 1921; Count Alexei Tolstoy remained a popular novelist.

Anatol Lunacharsky, a highly cultivated man who became the first Commissar of Education, did his best to graft the culture of the past on to the new Communist state. He took under his wing the Moscow Art Theatre, the Bolshoi and the Mariinsky, and reassured the performers, who were threatening to strike, that their role was no less important played before the people than before the Imperial Court. He recognized genius when he saw it, and found important employment for Kandinsky and Chagall. But the nationalization in July 1918 of the Moscow and Petrograd conservatoires and of all publishing houses, to say nothing of the total disappearance of private patrons, was inimical to the way of life of most creative artists, and a great cultural exodus began. The list of exiles included Stravinsky and Prokofiev themselves for a time, and even Gorky, as well as Rachmaninov, Chaliapin, Chagall, Kandinsky and Horowitz. A new artistic generation was left to flourish gaudily like seed sown on stony ground, and then to perish under the hot, destructive glare of 'socialist realism'.

By the autumn of 1918, wrote Galina von Meck in her diary, 'the thick curtains that had once adorned the windows of Moscow's residential district were cut up to make warm footwear for the winter. With shawls about their heads, women tramped the streets of the city to barter the few belongings still left to them for such food as they could get. Life was hard and wretched and full of hatred. The miracle was that a feeling of hope persisted. Many continued to believe that order would be restored and that Russia would return to normal.

'Every property-owner tried to fill his house with relatives and friends and to choose somebody decent as chairman of the house committee.

'Fuel was so scarce that we had to replace our large stoves by small ones with long iron pipes. In these we burned furniture, paper, and, later, the wooden fences between the houses. It was pathetic to see former grand mansions with strange tangles of iron chimneys poking out of the windows, all belching forth smoke in colours that varied according to the type of fuel being used.'[12]

By the following spring, wrote Gorky, 'during the first warm days, weird, fantastic people crawled out of the streets of Petrograd. Where and how had they lived hitherto? Doubtless in some slum, in old, solitary, crumbling houses, hidden away from life, insulted and rejected by the world. One dominant thought cropped up in my mind every time I saw them; they have forgotten something and are trying to recall it, silently crawling about the town in search of it.

'They were dressed in worn-out, tattered clothes, they were dirty and evidently very hungry, but they did not look like beggars and did not ask for alms. Very silently, very carefully, they walked along, watching the ordinary passers-by with suspicion and curiosity. As they stopped before the shop-windows they examined the things exhibited there with the eyes of folk who are trying to discover – or remember – what use one made of all those things. Motor-cars terrified them, as they terrified country men and women twenty years ago.'[13]

The last flicker of co-operation between the Bolshevik dictatorship and the survivors of the old regime occurred as late as July 1921. The New Economic Policy was then in full swing and there was famine in the eastern provinces of European Russia. The need for foreign aid was obvious, and a decree was published establishing an All-Russian Committee for Aid to the Hungry. Two former ministers of the Provisional Government, Kishkin and Prokopovich, along with some other well-known Cadets, were surprised to find themselves invited to join it. Their task was to collect supplies in Russia and abroad, and see to their distribution.

Unfortunately, the émigré Russian Press seized on this step as proof that the Soviet regime was crumbling; the

The news of the overthrow of the Autocracy reaches the front

After the February Revolution, all Tsarist emblems were removed

ВОСКРЕСЕНСКАЯ АПТЕКА

One of the many dispossessed by the Revolution;
General Seliveroff became a news-seller

British representative in Moscow made direct contact with
the Committee; and there was a general tendency abroad
to regard it as the nucleus of an alternative government. As
soon as the Soviet authorities reached an agreement with
Hoover's American Relief Administration, the Committee
became not only superfluous but dangerous from the Soviet
point of view. Its members were instructed to disperse and
organize relief independently in the stricken regions. When
in August the bourgeois members refused this mission, the
Committee was dissolved, and they were arrested.

12

The Scattering

The vagaries of the civil war and of the Allied interventions, the sheer size of the former empire, and, above all, the tendency of human beings, when not aroused, to continue in their familiar ways, all conspired to prolong the death agonies of the old Russia.

Some of the dispossessed could live on their fat longer than others. Early in 1918 the Grand Duke Paul, who escaped arrest longer than the rest of the Romanovs, abandoned his sumptuous palace at Tsarskoye Selo, not being able to afford to heat it; and his wife, Princess Paley, was given the job of conducting plebeian visitors round her former stately home and its now unkempt gardens. She and her husband took possession of a small *datcha* nearby, the property of the Grand Duke Boris. When Robien visited them there in February the Princess's son Vladimir opened the door to him, and helped him off with his coat. The guest joined a family meal with the children and governess. The Grand Duke had managed to save, from the rape of his cellar, some bottles of Mouton-Rothschild, one of which he proudly produced. The Princess had just lost her brother Valois, a popular theatrical producer, who had been murdered by a gang of ruffians on his way home from the theatre.

Vladimir, a gifted dilettante, had been amusing himself by writing a musical play about Cinderella, painting the scenery, and training fifty young ladies from the local lycée to perform it. 'The star turn', wrote Robien, 'is a ballet of violets and glow-worms. It is a pretty idea, if not very original.'[1]

A fashionable audience attended the performance, the officers wearing their epaulettes. 'One feels the monarchy here,' said Count Dimitri Scheremetiev to the Princess; 'we might almost be singing "God Save the Tsar".'[2]

It is difficult to reconcile this genteel picture of aristocratic patronage with the rising tide of horror all around. Yet the memoirs of the time, written by the literate of all classes, are full of such small occasions – family festivals, picnics, the chance meeting of old companions, flirtations, weddings, as well as the normal griefs of domestic life. Material comforts could no longer be taken for granted, and a warm room, a chicken, a smuggled bottle of vodka or the unexpected arrival of friends by the overcrowded public transport constituted in themselves a cause for celebration. Human nature is remarkably resilient, and great events do not always overshadow the significant small ones.

Civilized ways persisted in unlikely places. When Vladimir was banished and sent to live in an inn at Ekaterinburg, which he reached shortly after the Tsar had arrived there, he would walk round of an evening to the house of a regimental colleague to drink coffee and recite his poems to a small aristocratic circle. 'The Circle of the Green Lamp', he called it; 'a corner of the great Russia'. But in May he was transferred to a prison at Alapayesk, where, in common with five members of the Romanov family, he survived the Emperor by only one day.

His step-father, the Grand Duke Paul, did not escape arrest much longer. After his detention Princess Paley was advised to seek the help of Gorky, who was then installed in a luxurious Petrograd flat. The great man received her in bed, explaining that he was suffering from bronchitis.

'Beside him the celebrated singer Chaliapin was seated, with his big clean-shaven face, round and rubicund, – this Chaliapin who had had his Paris début at a concert in our house at Boulogne-sur-Seine, along with the Russian company led by Serge Diaghilev. He greeted me coldly and kept silent during the whole of my conversation with Gorky.'[3]

Gorky promised to intercede on the Grand Duke's behalf, but did not conceal the difficulties and obstacles he would meet.

'When I left, Chaliapin followed me into the next room. There, suddenly becoming communicative and kindly, he took my hands in his, kissed them, and said: "Princess, I must see you. Can I call tomorrow? I want to convince you that Chaliapin is not ungrateful and remembers what he owes to the grand duke his protector."

'He came next day to me at my sister Marianne's, drank a bottle of Madeira, and promised marvels of protection for "his grand duke". He had not enough insults for the Bolshevik regime.'[4]

But the Princess was disappointed. She recorded that Chaliapin did not lift a little finger to save the Grand Duke, and she described the great singer as 'an opportunist who prostrates himself before regicides as formerly he did before the Emperor and the imperial family'.[5]

The one Petrograd restaurant where, at a price, good food could still be had under Bolshevik rule was Donon's, which, being patronized by Count Mirbach and his newly arrived German mission, was given a specially privileged catering allowance. Allied diplomatists frequented it too for luncheon, so that the atmosphere was liable to become strained.

Because of bandits, the streets were too dangerous for dining out after dark, although the intrepid Countess Kleinmichel, now freed from house-arrest at the instance of Sazonov, was still to be seen in her two-horse carriage, visiting her remaining friends. At seventy-five, she declared, she saw little difference between being murdered in the street and waiting to be murdered at home. She escaped from Russia in 1921.

Peresash, which we have seen to be a model estate in the good old days, became a fortified camp when serious trouble broke out in the Ukraine. Several factors made this possible. Most of its employees already owned a stone house, a garden, a horse and a cow, and more than forty of the families were foreigners, chiefly Poles, who had no claim to Russian land and would have lost their homes and employment had the estate been broken up. Moreover, the nearest railway was many miles away, which meant that regular Bolshevik troops, as distinct from local bands, would be unlikely, for the time being, to disturb its peace.

So Vladimir Korostovetz, acting in the spirit of the new times, handed over the management of the estate to a workers' committee and, profiting from a legal right stemming from the possession of a distillery, provided it with arms for defence. Patrols were organized, which he joined as an ordinary member.

However, a feature of the civil war was that the worst excesses occurred during periods of interregnum, when the peasantry tended to take matters into their own hands. Both the Whites and the Reds attempted to maintain some kind of order, but whenever there was a vacuum anything could happen.

Thus, when the treaty of Brest-Litovsk allowed the Germans to occupy the Ukraine and the local Bolsheviks fled, the relative peace of that region was rudely shattered by the local peasantry. Vladimir Korostovetz rode over to his neighbours the Komarovsky family, whose hospitality, in happier days, has been described in Chapter 2.

'I found the whole family sitting quietly after lunch, and they began telling me with the greatest joy that at last the Germans had arrived and anarchy would be at an end. But as I was too well aware of the state of mind of the peasants I did my best to persuade them to move into town, explaining that, as now the peasants were not legally incited to loot, they would begin to commit robbery and violence on their own account. But old Komarovsky began to give me the most idyllic description of the peasants' love for him and how they would never injure him.'[6]

Two days later the Komarovskys, their two married daughters, a son-in-law and two militiamen who had happened to be staying with them were murdered in the most brutal circumstances.

When the Germans came and took possession of the area 'it was a terrible scene that met our eyes. The corpses were all bent and deformed, each with eight or ten bullet wounds, the bodies loathsomely mutilated, the heads battered to pulp, surrounded by pools of coagulated blood. Paraffin lamps were smoking, tables and chairs were overturned, and vodka and wine spilled all over.

'The house and farm servants greeted me obsequiously, expressing their sorrow about the "poor masters". But when they were asked who had done it nobody would reply.

'I know for a fact that the Komarovskys were kind and humane landowners who did no end of good for the peasants. The poor could always be certain of obtaining firewood from them, or timber for building, while land was rented to them for a purely nominal sum.'[7]

'Fort Peresash' was now in danger, and the Germans, without consulting its owners, sent a small detachment of Junkers and Ukrainian Cossacks for its protection.

'This was not an unmitigated blessing, for I soon had an opportunity to convince myself that the Revolution had morally degenerated officers and intelligentsia as well. The greater part of the detachment consisted of youthful students in various exotic uniforms of their own invention; the uniforms were certainly the outward and visible sign of submission, but their wearers feared danger like the plague. They were never equal to the slightest difficulty, and in dealing with the population they adopted a defiant attitude because they looked upon themselves as masters. Apart from this they were notable for their insolence, boasting and drunkenness, as well as the most utter disregard of the personal property of those whom they had been sent to protect. The presence of these people in Peresash quite destroyed our unity, which had already weathered so many storms, and I immediately began to take steps to have them removed from our midst.'[8]

Later, when the Germans had established the Hetman Skoropadsky as military dictator of the Ukraine, Korostovetz tried to recruit unemployed officers in Kiev to strengthen his defensive garrison.

'I noticed that many of these, even though belonging to the better classes, had not been left untouched by the moral degeneration. When inspecting night watches, I would often notice that officers had simply left their posts and lain down to sleep.'[9]

Peace returned under the Germans, and in the summer of 1918 Milyukov came to stay at Peresash, under the borrowed name of Professor Ivanov.

'In the idyllic surroundings of country life he worked hard at his book on the Russian Revolution as though this were already a matter of history, playing the violin to my wife's accompaniment in the intervals of his work. A great event during his visit was the discovery of a number of tumuli of the races that lived in our part of the country long before the Christian era. Every time an urn was brought to light Milyukov would make a long speech about the customs and burial ceremonies of the ancient Scythians. This idyll was once rather spoiled by the gardener Miron who helped in the digs; he asked why the professor was so interested in skulls and spent so much time writing about them instead of helping us to keep watch in the orchards where raiders were difficult to keep away.

'Other "unslaughtered bourgeois" who arrived included Prince G. N. Trubezkoy and my uncle Korostovetz, former Minister to Persia and China. After their experiences in "Sovdepia" the peace and quiet reigning in Peresash appeared to them like a fairy tale.'[10]

In the autumn of 1918 Korostovetz again visited Kiev, where he found 'a feeling of careless happiness' enlivened by national costume and the Ukrainian language.

'At night illuminated entrances to cabarets, theatres and other places of entertainment were visible everywhere. There were the Commercial Club, the Château des Fleurs, the Hotel Continental, the restaurants Semadini and François, as well as the newly opened Rus and the roof garden Praga. In the last the guests were waited on by officers wearing military distinctions, a sight that impressed me more than painfully, for it proved to me once more how little the situation was realized by the intelligentsia and aristocracy. They did not enter the service of the Hetman and therefore missed their last opportunity for organizing themselves during this lull in the storm.'[11]

The number of educated people among the Ukrainian nationalists was small, and so the responsible posts had to be filled by Russian bureaucrats and landowners, who looked on this work as purely temporary and as a chance for making money in various ways.

'They hated the Ukraine, the Germans and the Hetman, and were only waiting for everything to collapse and a new Russia to arise, a new empire like that which had existed under the Romanovs for three hundred years. They could not understand the underlying reasons for the Revolution, and could not grasp the fact that life, like a river, cannot flow backwards.'[12]

In Kiev, Korostovetz often met people in the streets who had managed to escape from 'Sovdepia' disguised as German or Austrian prisoners of war. 'Only a few days after escaping the horrors of Bolshevism they would begin loudly to criticize the Hetman, his Government, the Ukrainian language and the Germans.'

Before leaving Kiev, Korostovetz met Milyukov again, with the leader of the Cadets in the city, Grigorovitch Barsky.

'I imagined that at least among the liberals there would be people with enough sense to recognize the situation and, besides criticizing, would be able to make some valuable suggestions. But here too I met only with the psychology of parliamentary opposition which was dreaming of returning to power. In the name of the resuscitation of a united Russia, Milyukov was working hard to enter into relations with the Germans.'[13]

The chaos that followed the German withdrawal from the Ukraine after the Armistice ended with the arrival in force of the Red Army. 'Fort Peresash', though it was proof against any kind of local lawlessness, could not, of course, expect to withstand an organized military force. On New Year's Day 1919, therefore, the family paid six months' wages to the staff and handed over the estate to its internal soviet, in the vain hope that this body would be able to come to terms with the new authorities. Then they slipped away and went into hiding. Vladimir and his wife, before reaching the safety of the Polish frontier seven months later, had many adventures, but his mother, that very progressive Lady Bountiful, was arrested and shot along with his older brother, while his younger brother, on being discovered by the Bolsheviks, fought bravely and then turned the last cartridge on himself.

The fecklessness that Korostovetz observed in Kiev was apparent all over Russia in the mushroom states that rose and fell under foreign protection during the civil war. After the Armistice of November 1918 the counter-revolution lost any kind of moral coherence. The Allied interventionists – British, French, American, Italian, Japanese – began to play different games once Germany was defeated, and the old Russian ruling classes on whom they were relying to help them destroy the Bolsheviks were so obviously concerned with regaining their property and privileges that they failed to mobilize the anti-Bolshevik sentiments of the peasant masses. The more socially conscious of the bourgeoisie had already joined the Revolution, and were being destroyed by it. The Cadet Party was no longer even a moral force, having thrown up the sponge and opted for individual action in favour of a temporary military dictatorship. The counter-revolution, therefore, was entirely dependent on the whims of hypocritical foreigners. As the invaders withdrew, the White armies were defeated one by one, under Yudenich in the west, Kolchak in the east, Kornilov, Denikin and Wrangel in the south. The way was clear for the Red Army to break up one fragile political organization after another and lay the foundations of the totalitarian Union of Soviet Socialist Republics we know today.

The fate of Odessa provided perhaps the most terrible example of what could happen to White Russians who put their trust in the Allies. In March 1919 this great seaport was under the protection of 70,000 French troops, and seemed perfectly secure, since the force opposed to it consisted only of 15,000 ill-armed Reds under the Cossack turncoat Nikofar Grigorev. The city was sheltering half a million refugees, and Prince Lobanov-Rostovsky, who was present as a liaison officer with the French forces, described the atmosphere as 'merry and carefree', notwithstanding the overcrowding and the consequent epidemic of typhus. Galloping inflation was causing people to spend their money recklessly; hence there was an enormous growth of places of entertainment. At night, on the main thoroughfares, which were brilliantly lit, holiday crowds surged, cafés did a roaring trade and first-class shows were put on in the cabarets by refugee entertainers.

One evening Lobanov went to the opera to see *Madam Butterfly*. 'As is usual in Russia, the settings were gorgeous. The vast opera house was crowded by elegantly dressed people, giving the impression that the clock had been set back two years.'[14]

But all was not well. Kiev had fallen to the Bolsheviks without a struggle on 3 February, and Grigorev was advancing towards the Black Sea. The French troops, now that the struggle against Germany was over, had no intention of engaging in serious hostilities against a people with whom their own country was not at war and in support of a mass of refugees who held them in scant respect.

Suddenly, on 29 March, there was a change of policy in Paris, and on 2 April an announcement appeared in the Odessa newspapers stating that, because of difficulties in supplying the city, the French forces would withdraw within the next seventy-two hours to lessen the number of mouths to feed. Panic ensued as civilians fought for places in the departing ships. Men, women and children were trampled to death, or were drowned as they fell, or were pushed, off the crowded quays.

The French navy succeeded in evacuating 30,000 civilians and 10,000 members of the Volunteer Army. But, as Robert Jackson has described it: 'As the last ships pulled out a great silence fell on the crowds who had clung in hope and despair to the quaysides until the very last moment. Whole families prayed together, then committed suicide. It was a sight that would remain with the French soldiers for the rest of their lives.'[15]

The fall of Odessa was followed by the Allied evacuation of the Crimea, where a pale shadow of aristocratic life had persisted in the splendid seaside palaces. Among those who made good their escape in a British warship were the Empress Dowager and the Grand Duke Nicholas.

The intervention continued its erratic course, and nearly a year later the tragedy of Odessa was repeated at Novorossisk, when it was evacuated by the British. They had room to take with them only those civilians who had been actively engaged in the White cause. The rest had to be kept back by troops with fixed bayonets; and civilians who broke this cordon were machine-gunned.

Another example of betrayal was Baku, which we last observed as all classes there joyfully welcomed the February Revolution. The political honeymoon did not last long. Mayor Bych became a 'March socialist' and the local Cadets gradually lost influence. Events in distant Petrograd and Moscow were reflected by the Caspian Sea, and in April 1918 Baku's liberal and Menshevik newspapers were suppressed. A Committee of Revolutionary Defence, led by the local Bolshevik hero Shaumian, supplanted the city duma as the organ of municipal government.

Yet Shaumian was unable to nationalize the oil industry, on whose production the Central Government depended. All he could do was to levy a 50 million rouble tax on it. He confiscated the splendid villas of the tycoons on the Marine Boulevard, but allowed them to continue to live there on payment of exorbitant rents. He also appointed commissars to share in the direction of the private steamship companies, and disbanded the aristocratic Naval Flying School.

The Baku Bolsheviks were physically isolated from the Government in Moscow, and were free to manage their own affairs. In May they established the 'Baku Commune', and attempted to reproduce locally the political organizations of the Centre, including a Council of People's Commissars. They failed, however, to reorganize the schools and the courts on Communist lines.

The result was that, when British forces entered the town in July in support of the Nationalist Government of Azerbaijan, its pre-revolutionary economic and social structure was still more or less intact. The Commissars were shipped to Krasnovodsk, across the Caspian, where they were shot by another group of Whites. There were many political changes of fortune after that, but at the end of 1919 the British finally evacuated Baku, trusting that Azerbaijan's independence was assured by the recent Soviet Declaration of the Rights of Nationalities. This enabled the Eleventh Soviet Army to enter the town on 20 April 1920, without resistance, and arrest and shoot the entire Azerbaijan Government.

A Cheka officer, Evgeny Dumbadze, who later escaped to France to avoid a purge, described what happened next. The Red forces were let loose on the town for twenty-four hours, on the understanding that they would amuse themselves only at the expense of the bourgeoisie. Well-to-do homes were looted, convents were robbed, young women from prominent families were raped and nuns were forced to dance naked before being raped and shot. Many citizens were killed with bayonets and knives, or incinerated in their burning houses.

After the troops had returned to their barracks, the Cheka appeared on the streets. All officers of the National Azerbaijan Army were gaoled, along with government employees down to harbour masters, station masters and postal officials, with their wives and families. Over the space of six days these prisoners were transferred in two small steamboats to the nearby Nargen Island, where they were mown down by machineguns in groups of a hundred. This Dumbadze described as 'the week of the suppression of the bourgeoisie'.

But Prince Lobanov-Rostovsky, when he was attached to General Denikin's headquarters at Taganrog, noted how quickly bourgeois life came back to normal when the enemy front was stabilized at some distance away.

'The healing process seemed to be as rapid in social life as in the case of physical wounds, and the everyday routine with its petty interests made people forget all past miseries and tribulations. Taganrog was fast assuming the aspect of a little capital, or a parody of one. Administration became more and more complex with an appearance of permanence. The crack regiments of the Volunteer Army, composed solely of former officers, the Kornilov, Martov and Drosdov Regiments, were assuming the place of the former Imperial Guards. The numerous foreign military missions – the large

British Mission, the French, Italian, Serbian, Rumanian, Bulgarian and Japanese – were filling the role of embassies and legations. Social life started, notwithstanding the squalid and overcrowded quarters in which people were living. Baroness Nolken had a "day", and members of the foreign missions visited these receptions assiduously. Countess Hendrikov gave little parties at which the British were lionized by Russian ladies. On Thursday evenings the excellent headquarters symphony orchestra gave concerts in the local theatre. With all foreign missions present and the ladies dressing up to the limited means available there was a certain show of elegance. Dinner parties and banquets followed one another. All kinds of foreign notables began visiting Taganrog, and there was a real flurry of excitement when a member of the House of Savoy, Prince Udine, arrived on an Italian cruiser. Questions of etiquette, seating charts, and so on occupied our whole attention that day, and the Civil War was forgotten.'[16]

Not for long, though. Taganrog fell to the Reds at Christmas 1919. After Wrangel's evacuation of the Crimea, armed resistance to the Bolsheviks collapsed.

In the civil war more people perished through famine, disease and reprisals than in the fighting. Richard Luckett thought the total number of deaths could be 25 million. Some 500,000 persons were killed by the Cheka, and about the same number by the White security forces.

The Whites failed politically, and never did more than set up fantasy regimes in the areas which, at various times, they controlled. This bore out Lenin's theory, completing Paléologue's, that the only alternative to Communist dictatorship was a return to the Tsarist regime. This, by the time the Whites took the field, was politically impossible.

The last chapter in the story of the propertied classes of the old Russia is a fragmented one of individual loss of identity, privation, imprisonment or death, or of escape in an infinite variety of circumstances. By 1922 there were estimated to be 860,000 White Russian refugees in Europe, the Far East and Asia Minor. A large colony of them was established in Shanghai, which proved to be only a temporary refuge from Communism. Only about half the exiles found a permanent home; the rest have had to keep on moving, from Hitler's Germany, from Nazi-occupied Europe or from Mao's China.

A new element was added to the *dramatis personae* of romantic novelists and scenario-writers, as represented by the prince who drove a Paris taxi, the countess who became an adventuress in the Levant, or the aide-de-camp general who died in poverty, fingering his medals and gazing at a portrait of the Tsar. Most of the exiles, however, had, by western middle-class standards, been quite ordinary people in their previous lives. Their only fault had been that they had held aloof from the Revolution in its latter stages. Had they embraced it, their fate might have been even worse.

The politicians among them drifted naturally to the larger cities, liberals like Milyukov and Social-Revolutionaries like Tseretelli to Paris and Prague, conservatives to Berlin and Belgrade. There they spent their leisure in endlessly mulling over the events of the past and writing their own self-justificatory versions of them. To what they had been looking forward most of their lives, either with joyful expectation or with dread, they now looked back. They had moved from one phase of unreality into another, and the reality in between made them shudder.

General Wrangel tried to maintain the cadre structure of the Volunteer Army in exile. With the Grand Duke Nicholas he formed the R.O.V.S., or World Organization of Russian War Veterans, which at least was able to help provide for the destitute.

For a time, and for some of the exiles, Hitler's invasion of the Soviet Union revived either their patriotism or their personal ambitions. Those living in the Reich who trusted the Nazis, of all people, to put the Russian clock back joined a specially formed 'Cossack' force under General Krasnov, formerly Ataman of the Don; those in occupied Bulgaria, Rumania, Yugoslavia and Greece joined the Rogozhin Group, and dressed up once more in the uniforms of the old imperial army. But the end of the Second World War brought further migrations and many unwilling re-patriations, including that of Krasnov, who was hanged.

The United States, where Kerensky had established himself, became the chief centre for exiled reminiscences and recrimination.

The Grand Duke Cyril, after the massacre of so many of his relatives, became unexpectedly the head of the Romanov family. He had been the first member of his clan to renounce his oath of allegiance and embrace the Revolution. Now, from the safety of France, he had the impudence to proclaim himself rightful Tsar of all the Russias. The Empress Dowager, from her refuge in Denmark, refused to recognize his title, and the House of Romanov remained divided to the last.

The people with whom this book deals – the whole body of the Russian possessing classes who either died, went into exile or lost their identity among the masses during the Revolution – are referred to by official Soviet historians as 'former persons'. They are not regarded as constituting a link in an historical chain. In the Bolshevik view this was effectively broken in 1917, which enables subsequent writers to take a highly selective view of pre-revolutionary Russian history.

It is indeed true that the last generation of leaders of the Tsarist Empire have left no observable legacy in their homeland, now the Union of Soviet Socialist Republics. That so large and influential a group should have been without political or social posterity must be an event unique in the history of mankind. The group included not only purblind supporters of an anachronistic autocracy but men who had spent a lifetime considering how to modify or destroy it; not only the selfishly privileged but those whose concern had been to bridge the gap between two distinct societies. With them disappeared those whom the Bolsheviks described as 'petty-bourgeois', the new classes who, if Russian capitalism had been allowed to develop on western lines, would themselves have had an historic role to play. The Mensheviks and the Social-Revolutionaries have all in their turn been thrown into Trotsky's 'rubbish heap of history', to be followed, indeed, during Stalin's purges, not only by the 'Old Bolsheviks' but by rank on rank of new party members and Red Army generals. The Soviet Union between the wars was a *tabula rasa* over which the plane passed more than once.

An account of the moral defects of Russian liberalism cannot of itself make sense of what happened. Some interpretation is needed of all the forces that came into play during the Revolution, whether it be in the form of a Marxist-Leninist analysis or not. The one clear lesson of those fateful years is that no social order dare make too many easy assumptions about its chances of survival, or even about its susceptibility to reform.

Notes

Notes

Preface
1. Maurice Paléologue, *An Ambassador's Memoirs* (Hutchinson, 1973), p. 798.
2. Konstantin Paustovsky, *In That Dawn* (Harvill Press, 1967), p. 41.

Chapter 2 : Men of Property
1. Countess Kleinmichel, *Memories of a Shipwrecked World* (Brentano, 1923), p. 222.
2. Maurice Paléologue, *An Ambassador's Memoirs* (Hutchinson, 1973), p. 431.
3. Count Lucien de Robien, *Diary of a Diplomat in Russia* (Michael Joseph, 1969), p. 118.
4. Countess Kleinmichel, *op cit.*, p. 134.
5. Sir Robert Bruce Lockhart, *The Two Revolutions* (Phoenix House, 1957), p. 44.
6. Vladimir Korostovetz, *Seed and Harvest* (Faber, 1931), p. 121.
7. Maxim Gorky, *Fragments From My Diary* (Allen Lane, 1972), p. 232.
8. Maxim Gorky, *op cit.*, p. 250.
9. Maxim Gorky, *op cit.*, p. 235.

Chapter 3: War

1. Sir Bernard Pares, *My Russian Memoirs* (Cape, 1931), p. 513.
2. Vladimir Korostovetz, *Seed and Harvest* (Faber, 1931), p. 210.
3. Countess Kleinmichel, *Memories of a Shipwrecked World* (Brentano, 1923), p. 217.
4. Prince A. Lobanov-Rostovsky, *The Grinding Mill* (Macmillan, 1935), p. 167.
5. Maurice Paléologue, *An Ambassador's Memoirs* (Hutchinson, 1973), p. 447.
6. L. D. Trotsky, *History of the Russian Revolution*, vol. I (Gollancz, 1932), p. 84.
7. L. D. Trotsky, *op. cit.*, vol. I, p. 45.
8. Camilla Gray, *The Russian Experiment in Art 1863–1922* (Thames and Hudson, 1971), p. 186.
9. Maurice Paléologue, *An Ambassador's Memoirs* (Hutchinson, 1973), p. 755.
10. L. D. Trotsky, *op. cit.*, vol. I, p. 95.
11. Maurice Paléologue, *op. cit.*, p. 808.
12. Vladimir Korostovetz, *op. cit.*, p. 211.

Chapter 4: February 1917

1. Nicholas Sukhanov, *The Russian Revolution 1917* (Oxford University Press, 1955), p. 3.
2. Maurice Paléologue, *An Ambassador's Memoirs* (Hutchinson, 1973), p. 860.
3. Maurice Paléologue, *op. cit.*, p. 824.
4. Maurice Paléologue, *op. cit.*, p. 860.
5. Countess Kleinmichel, *Memories of a Shipwrecked World* (Brentano, 1923), p. 230.
6. Aleksei Tarasov-Rodianov, *February 1917* (Covici Friede, New York, 1931), p. 107.
7. Nicholas Sukhanov, *op. cit.*, p. 88.
8. Aleksei Tarasov-Rodianov, *op. cit.*, p. 107.
9. Countess Kleinmichel, *op. cit.*, p. 236.
10. Countess Kleinmichel, *op. cit.*, p. 238.
11. Countess Kleinmichel, *op. cit.*, p. 197.
12. Kschessinska, *Dancing in Petersburg* (Gollancz, 1960), p. 163.

13. Kschessinska, *op. cit.*, p. 164.
14. Kschessinska, *op. cit.*, p. 166.
15. Maurice Paléologue, *op. cit.*, p. 822.
16. Princess Zinaida Shakhovskoi, *The Privilege was Mine* (Cape, 1959), p. 11.
17. Princess Zinaida Shakhovskoi, *op. cit.*, p. 12.
18. E. M. Almedingen, *Tomorrow Will Come* (Bodley Head, 1941), p. 13.
19. Sir Robert Bruce Lockhart, *The Two Revolutions* (Phoenix House, 1957), p. 75.

Chapter 5: 'In That Dawn'
1. Marylie Markovitch, *La Révolution Russe* (Perrin, Paris, 1918). p. 78.
2. *ibid.*
3. Maurice Paléologue, *An Ambassador's Memoirs* (Hutchinson, 1973), p. 839.
4. Nicholas Sukhanov, *The Russian Revolution 1917* (Oxford University Press, 1955), p. 198.
5. Konstantin Paustovsky, *op. cit.*, p. 10.
6. A. F. Kerensky, *Memoirs* (Cassell, 1966), p. 227.
7. Count Lucien de Robien, *Diary of a Diplomat in Russia* (Michael Joseph, 1969), p. 22.
8. Maurice Paléologue, *op. cit.*, p. 858.
9. Maurice Paléologue, *op. cit.*, p. 848.
10. Maurice Paléologue, *op. cit.*, p. 866.
11. Maurice Paléologue, *op. cit.*, p. 867.
12. Prince A. Lobanov-Rostovsky, *The Grinding Mill* (Macmillan, 1935), p. 201.
13. *ibid.*
14. Prince A. Lobanov-Rostovsky, *op. cit.*, p. 204.
15. Prince A. Lobanov-Rostovsky, *op. cit.*, p. 208.
16. *ibid.*
17. Maurice Paléologue, *op. cit.*, p. 878.
18. *ibid.*
19. Vladimir Korostovetz, *Seed and Harvest* (Faber, 1931), p. 279.
20. Nicholas Sukhanov, *op. cit.*, p. 77.
21. Elisaveta Fen, *Remember Russia* (Hamish Hamilton, 1973), p. 74.

22. Boris Pasternak, *Dr Zhivago* (Fontana, 1961), p. 174.

Chapter 6: Dyarchy
1. Count Lucien de Robien, *Diary of a Diplomat in Russia* (Michael Joseph, 1969), p. 33.
2. *ibid.*
3. Count Lucien de Robien, *op. cit.*, p. 42.
4. Maurice Paléologue, *An Ambassador's Memoirs* (Hutchinson, 1973), p. 902.
5. Countess Kleinmichel, *Memories of a Shipwrecked World* (Brentano, 1923), p. 259.
6. Princess Zinaida Shakhovskoi, *The Privilege was Mine* (Cape, 1959,) p. 13.
7. Sir Bernard Pares, *My Russian Memoirs* (Cape, 1931), p. 458.
8. Prince A. Lobanov-Rostovsky, *The Grinding Mill* (Macmillan, 1935), p. 230.
9. *ibid.*
10. *ibid.*
11. *ibid.*
12. L. D. Trotsky, *History of the Russian Revolution*, vol. I (Gollancz, 1932), p. 344.
13. Maurice Paléologue, *op. cit.*, p. 921.
14. *ibid.*
15. Sir Robert Bruce Lockhart, *The Two Revolutions* (Phoenix House, 1957), p. 45.
16. Maurice Paléologue, *op. cit.*, p. 925.

Chapter 7: Coalition
1. Nicholas Sukhanov, *The Russian Revolution 1917* (Oxford University Press, 1955), p. 379.
2. L. D. Trotsky, *History of the Russian Revolution*, vol. I (Gollancz, 1932), p. 455.
3. *ibid.*
4. Nicholas Sukhanov, *op. cit.*, p. 348.
5. Nicholas Sukhanov, *op. cit.*, p. 362.
6. Nicholas Sukhanov, *op. cit.*, p. 379.
7. Nicholas Sukhanov, *op. cit.*, p. 410.

Chapter 8: A. F. Kerensky

1. L. D. Trotsky, *History of the Russian Revolution*, vol. II (Gollancz, 1932), p. 132.
2. L. D. Trotsky, *op. cit.*, vol. II, p. 202.
3. Sir Robert Bruce Lockhart, *The Two Revolutions*, (Phoenix House, 1957), p. 104.

Chapter 9: The Abyss

1. Nicholas Sukhanov, *The Russian Revolution* (Oxford University Press, 1955), p. 518.
2. *ibid.*
3. L. D. Trotsky, *History of the Russian Revolution*, vol. III (Gollancz, 1932), p. 37.
4. John Reed, *Ten Days that Shook the World* (Penguin, 1966), p. 38.
5. *ibid.*
6. John Reed, *op. cit.*, p. 40.
7. M. Philips Price, *My Reminiscences of the Russian Revolution* (George, Allen and Unwin, 1921), p. 104.
8. *ibid.*
9. M. Philips Price, *op. cit.*, p. 108.
10. M. Philips Price, *op. cit.*, p. 109.
11. M. Philips Price, *op. cit.*, p. 112.
12. M. Philips Price, *op. cit.*, p. 114.
13. John Reed, *op. cit.*, p. 61.
14. Count Lucien de Robien, *Diary of a Diplomat in Russia* (Michael Joseph, 1969), p. 116.
15. L. D. Trotsky, *op. cit.*, vol. III, p. 198.

Chapter 10: October 1917

1. John Reed, *Ten Days that Shook the World* (Penguin, 1966), p. 117.
2. John Reed, *op. cit.*, p. 190.
3. Vladimir Korostovetz, *Seed and Harvest* (Faber, 1931), p. 307.
4. Korostovetz, *op. cit.*, p. 299.
5. M. Philips Price, *My Reminiscences of the Russian Revolution* (George, Allen and Unwin, 1921), p. 207.
6. Boris Pasternak, *Dr Zhivago* (Fontana, 1961), p. 194.

7. Wictor Woroszycski, *The Life of Mayakovsky* (Gollancz, 1972), p. 202.
8. Wictor Woroszycski, *op. cit.*, p. 203.
9. Wictor Woroszycski, *op. cit.*, p. 194.
10. Wictor Woroszycski, *op. cit.*, p. 192.
11. Count Lucien de Robien, *Diary of a Diplomat in Russia* (Michael Joseph, 1969), p. 142.
12. Count Lucien de Robien, *op. cit.*, p. 177.
13. Count Lucien de Robien, *op. cit.*, p. 185.
14. Count Lucien de Robien, *op. cti.*, p. 186.
15. Galina von Meck, *As I Remember Them* (Dennis Dobson, 1973), p. 159.
16. Princess Shakhovskoi, *The Privilege was Mine* (Cape 1959), p. 14.

Chapter 11 : Bolshevism
1. Count Lucien de Robien, *Diary of a Diplomat in Russia* (Michael Joseph, 1969), p. 217.
2. Count Lucien de Robien, *op. cit.*, p. 229.
3. Sir Paul Vinogradov, *Encyclopaedia Britannica*, 12th edition, vol. XXXIII (1922), p. 319.
4. Count Lucien de Robien, *op. cit.*, p. 214.
5. Count Lucien de Robien, *op. cit.*, p. 272.
6. Count Lucien de Robien, *op. cit.*, p. 274.
7. M. Philips Price, *My Reminiscences of the Russian Revolution* (George, Allen and Unwin, 1921), p. 333.
8. M. Philips Price, *op. cit.*, p. 334.
9. *ibid.*
10. Prince A. Lobanov-Rostovsky, *The Grinding Mill* (Macmillan, 1935), p. 322.
11. Alexander Solzhenitsyn, *The Gulag Archipelago* (Collins, 1974), p. 28.
12. Galina von Meck, *As I Remember Them* (Dennis Dobson, 1973), p. 172.
13. Maxim Gorky, *Fragments From My Diary* (Allen Lane, 1972), p. 173.

Chapter 12 : The Scattering
1. Count Lucien de Robien, *Diary of a Diplomat in Russia* (Michael Joseph, 1969), p. 226.

2. Princess Paley, *Memories of Russia* (Jenkins, 1924), p. 240.
3. Princess Paley, *op. cit.*, p. 241.
4. *ibid.*
5. *ibid.*
6. Vladimir Korostovetz, *Seed and Harvest* (Faber, 1931), p. 328.
7. Vladimir Korostovetz, *op. cit.*, p. 333.
8. *ibid.*
9. Vladimir Korostovetz, *op. cit.*, p. 334.
10. Vladimir Korostovetz, *op. cit.*, p. 341.
11. Vladimir Korostovetz, *op. cit.*, p. 344.
12. Vladimir Korostovetz, *op. cit.*, p. 345.
13. Vladimir Korostovetz, *op. cit.*, p. 351.
14. Prince A. Lobanov-Rostovsky, *The Grinding Mill* (Macmillan, 1935), p. 331.
15. Robert Jackson, *At War with the Bolsheviks* (Tom Stacey, 1972), p. 176.
16. Prince A. Lobanov-Rostovsky, *op. cit.*, p. 356.

Index

Index

201